# Spiritual
# Meditations

# Spiritual Meditations

## AUGUST VAN RYN

### JOHN RITCHIE LTD
CHRISTIAN PUBLICATIONS

40 BEANSBURN, KILMARNOCK, SCOTLAND

ISBN 0 946351 63 5
Copyright 1997 by John Ritchie Ltd.
40 Beansburn, Kilmarnock, Scotland

Typeset by Newtext Composition Ltd., Glasgow
Printed by Bell and Bain Ltd., Glasgow

# Foreword

August Van Ryan was born in the Netherlands in May 1890. In 1907, along with his older brother Louis, he emigrated to the U.S.A. On 1st May 1910, while in Grand Rapids, Michigan, he was converted to Christ; this led him to engage in full-time ministry for His Lord in 1915.

Two years later, he received an invitation to visit the Bahamas and, while there, he met a young lady, Persis Melrose Roberts, whom he later married, and who became his worthy life-time partner. For almost fourteen years, along with Mr Robert Stratton, he sailed throughout the Bahamas spreading the gospel.

Fearing blindness, he memorised the New Testament and many portions of the Old Testament, which proved to be a great help to him in his christian service.

For over sixty years, he travelled throughout the United States, Canada and the Bahamas, preaching and teaching in assemblies of the Lord's people and at many of their conferences. He became a prolific writer of books, articles for magazines, and tracts. These have proved to be a real blessing to all who read them.

Shortly after the homecall of his beloved wife in July 1974, he completed the writing of his book "60 Years in His Service", after which, along with his older daughter Lorraine, he moved to Camp Shepherd Retirement Community for believers in Frostproof, Florida.

The Lord called Home peacefully this valiant servant on 24th February 1982. His desire for these hitherto unpublished meditations would have been that they now serve to bless and encourage the Lord's People, as we all await His joyous and imminent return for us.

# Preface

*"I knew a man in Christ, about fourteen years ago..."* It scarcely seems possible, but just a bit over fourteen years ago, in February 1982, my father was called Home in his 92nd year. "In Christ", he found his safety, security and satisfaction.

During 1995, as I was looking through Dad's old files, I discovered a thick folder which he had entitled "Homespun Homilies". It was a book that he had written but never published, consisting of random reflections on the Scriptures (accompanied by often humorous illustrations), thoughts he had gleaned in well over sixty years in the Lord's service.

We do not know at what point in his life he wrote these scattered thoughts, but believe that they can be a valuable help, challenge and encouragement to those who follow on to know the Lord, and to show Him to both believer and unbeliever.

Whether Dad intended these chapters to be published is not known to his family, but, in any case, it is possible that, through this legacy of words, he, through the Spirit, will both warm and warn the hearts of the Lord's dear people; and he, being dead (yet alive), may still speak to all.

Thanks are especially due to my dear wife, Joan, who so meticulously copied my father's faded, typed notes; and to all those who have had a part in their publication in one way or another.

July, 1996

Elliot M. Van Ryn
340 West 56th Street
Hialeah, FL 33012

# Contents

# Miracles for Human Needs

*"And the third day there was a marriage in Cana of Galilee; and the mother of Jesus was there: and both Jesus was called, and His disciples, to the marriage. And when they wanted (lacked) wine, the mother of Jesus saith unto Him, They have no wine...*

*"And there were set there six waterpots of stone, after the manner of the purifying of the Jews, containing two or three firkins apiece. Jesus saith unto them, Fill the waterpots with water. And they filled them up to the brim. And He saith unto them, Draw out now, and bear unto the governor of the feast. And they bare it. When the ruler of the feast had tasted the water that was made wine, and knew not whence it was: (but the servants which drew the water knew;) the governor of the feast called the bridegroom, and saith unto him, Every man at the beginning doth set forth good wine; and when men have well drunk, then that which is worse: but thou hast kept the good wine until now.*

*"This beginning of miracles did Jesus in Cana of Galilee..."*

*(John 2:1-3, 6-11)*

Moses' first miracle was to turn water into blood; Christ's first was to turn water into wine. In Moses' case, the result was death; in Christ's, it was life and joy. The first and last miracles performed by our Lord during His life on earth, as recorded in John's Gospel, were at a wedding and a funeral. He is that amazing Person who puts the joy into weddings and takes the sorrow out of funerals. Praise His Name!

Jesus is prominently seen at three weddings in the Scriptures. In the Garden of Eden, He was the "Best Man", in John 2, the Host; and in Revelation 19, the Bridegroom.

This miracle tells the story that joy runs out, even in married life. Here it ran out on the very wedding day, picturing how joy, typified by wine, often fails in real life. However, while joy usually does not fail on the wedding day, it will run out sometime. Life is not all picnic. In a flash flood, a husband was carried down the raging torrent clinging to a dining room table, while his wife accompanied him on the piano, but things are not always as harmonious as that. As one wife said to her husband after a few years of connubial bliss: "When you proposed to me, you promised to be humbly grateful if I accepted you, but you are, instead, grumbly hateful."

So, it pays to invite the Lord as a Guest to your wedding, and let Him take the place of the Host, as He did on this occasion. When our blessed Lord furnishes the wine, it is good to the last drop. When all earthly joys end, then "in His presence there is fulness of joy; and at His right hand there are pleasures for evermore" (Psalm 16:11).

# Worship

*"But the hour cometh, and now is, when the true worshippers shall worship the Father in spirit and in truth: for the Father seeketh such to worship Him. God is a Spirit: and they that worship Him must worship Him in spirit and in truth."*

(John 4:23-24)

Jesus said to this Gentile woman: "We know what we worship: for salvation is of the Jews". I wonder whether the emphasis here might be placed on that word "what". With the Jews, worship had largely degenerated into a "what" worship, in place of a "Whom". This thought is suggested by our Lord's words in Matthew 15:8: "This people draweth nigh unto Me with their mouth, and honoureth Me with their lips; but their heart is far from Me".

Nothing is easier than to slip from reality into formality; ritualism soon becomes rut-ualism. True worship is not worship of some thing, but of Some One, and that One is God the Father and Christ the Son. The true worshippers, says Jesus, worship the Father; and now that Jesus is risen and glorified, worship goes out to Him as well, as the Scriptures show.

That's why Jesus says here that true worshippers worship in spirit; not in the letter that killeth, but in the spirit which giveth life. True christian worship is not a certain set form or procedure, but it is the heart welling up to God in enraptured delight as, by faith, we know Him in all His greatness and glory.

A dear friend of mine likes to use the following illustration. Folks sometimes say to Him, "Brother, I am sorry I can't be with you tonight at the service, but I will be with you in spirit". He says it gives him the creeps to see all those disembodied spirits sitting on empty seats. But, there is something almost as bad, perhaps worse in God's sight, and that is to see disenspirited bodies sitting on full seats! Many a saint comes to the meeting and you have no difficulty seeing him there, for he sits there in his body as big as life, but if you could see as God sees, you would find out that he really isn't there at all. He's working at his job as a contractor, or perhaps he is having an argument with his boss; maybe he is busy figuring out his income tax; in short, he may be anywhere, but he isn't in church. Let's see to it that we worship the Lord in spirit as well as in truth. Beloved brother J. N. Darby knew something of this presence of body but absence of spirit when he wrote:

> "No infant's changing pleasure
> Is like my wandering mind".

It calls for real watchfulness and spiritual stamina to worship the Lord in spirit and in truth. We Christians sometimes boast of the vast knowledge God has given us of

His precious Word, and we have no doubt but that we worship in truth; but, alas, the spirit often is sorely lacking. "Set your mind on things above, where Christ sitteth on the right hand of God."

# Feeding the Multitude

*"When Jesus then lifted up His eyes, and saw a great company come unto Him, He saith unto Philip, Whence shall we buy bread, that these may eat? And this He said to prove him: for He Himself knew what He would do. Philip answered Him, Two hundred pennyworth of bread is not sufficient for them, that every one of them may take a little. One of His disciples, Andrew, Simon Peter's brother, saith unto Him, There is a lad here, which hath five barley loaves, and two small fishes: but what are they among so many?"*

(John 6:5-9)

We have all thrilled to the wonder of this miracle, which is the only one recorded in all the four gospels. We know that it tells forth the provision made for the souls of men through the precious work of Christ, through the Bread that was broken for us upon the Cross, so that sinners might eat and live forever.

There are many who reject the truth of the miracles performed by Christ and others, as recorded in the Scriptures. One such, a Sunday School teacher, told her class of boys that Jesus never did such a miracle. "Why," she said, "He was a man like other men - more holy, no doubt, but still only a man, and He could not do anything like that. What really happened," so she told her impressionable pupils, "was that Jesus spoke to those thousands of people, and He was such a fluent and forceful speaker that, when He got through with His speech, they all just felt filled; that's how it was." Up flew one little hand, and when its small owner was permitted to speak, he said: "Teacher, what filled the baskets?" Out of the mouth of a little babe, eh?

The Lord asked the question: "Where shall we buy bread?" Philip answered, "What with?" Andrew said, "For whom?" Neither listened to Christ. Philip looked at the cash, or lack of it; Andrew looked at the crowd, and neither of them looked at Christ. That's still the weakness in much christian service.

I guess Andrew had a weak sort of faith in Christ when he brought the lad with five small buns and two small fishes to the Lord and said, "What are they among so many?" He certainly knew that they were utterly insufficient to meet the need of five thousand men, beside women and children. Bringing him to Jesus, he seemed to feel that perhaps the Lord could do something with that small supply. He could, and He did. In fact, He could have fed that vast crowd without having anything at all to start with, for He made the worlds out of nothing in the first place. The use of this boy's lunch illustrates that our blessed Lord wants to use what we offer Him, and then add His blessing to it.

The story is told of a young preacher who was preaching his sermon before a critical audience. He took this incident for his text, but in his nervous excitement, he got things twisted a mite:

"Friends," said he, "I am going to speak to you this morning on how Jesus fed five men and women on five thousand loaves and two thousand fishes." "That's nothing," said a grumbly old deacon sitting on the front seat, "I can do that, too." The preacher made no reply, but went on with his discourse. The next Sunday, he took the same text and subject, and this time, speaking very slowly and deliberately, he said, "Friends, I am going to speak to you this morning on how our Lord fed five thousand men, beside women and children, on five loaves and two little fishes." And then, leaning far over the pulpit, he said to the old curmudgeon, "Brother Smith, can you do that, too?" "I sure can," was the startling reply. "You can?" asked the minister, in open astonishment, "How?" "With what was left over from last Sunday," came the convincing answer.

Yes, that's how it is with us, too. If we are to do great things, we have to have something to do them with, but not so our blessed Lord. He does not have to, but He does want to take our little and spread it far and wide by His power and grace.

That little lad could have done at least three things with his lunch: (1) he could have eaten it himself; and so Christians might live much, if not altogether, for self; (2) he might have distributed the loaves himself; in which case two or three people might have had a small bite each; so, too, we believers sometimes serve the Lord in our own strength and accomplish so little; or (3) he could have given his buns into the hands of Christ, which he did; and, to his utter amazement, his lunch was multiplied till it fed perhaps ten thousand souls, with still more left at the close than there was at the start.

Let us put our little, in deep dependence on the power and love of Christ, into His hands, and He will bless it so that many will be reached and blessed as they partake of the Bread of Life.

# Chosen to Bear Fruit

*"Ye have not chosen Me, but I have chosen you, and ordained you, that ye should go and bring forth fruit, and that your fruit should remain: that whatsoever ye shall ask of the Father in My Name, He may give it you."*

(John 15:16)

There is an election to salvation as set forth in Romans 8:33-34. That wonderful passage assures us that we are justified through the precious death of Christ for us, that He is risen and now lives at God's right hand to intercede for His own, so that He might save them to the uttermost, as Hebrews 7:25 tells us. We are God's elect; we are the elite of society; we belong to the "400", we are the multi-billionaires of heavenly riches.

You have heard the tale of the little girl who came home quite distressed. Her little playmate, in a fit of temper, had said to her: "You're nobody, anyway; you're not even born; you're just adopted." She asked her mother, "Am I, Mama? Am I adopted? What's adoption mean, Mommy?" The mother realized the hour had arrived to tell her little adopted daughter the whole story; so she did, in great detail. That afternoon, back at school, the little girl found her friend. "Now I know all about it," said she. "My mommy told me. She and my daddy did not have any children, and they wanted very badly a little girl. So, they went to all kinds of 'stutions, and one day they were in a big 'stution that had dozens of little baby girls in it. They picked out the very prettiest one they could find - that was me - and they took me home to be their little girl." And then, as a parting shot, she fired this one: "But you, your parents had to take what they got!"

Of course, we were not elected because we were the best. God chose us in infinite grace. He loves us because of who He is, for God is love. In anticipation, He saw us perfect in beauty, because of the beauty of His only Son, which He was going to put upon us. He could afford to choose the sinful and the ugly, because He could change all that. From all eternity, He had in mind the marvellous transformation His love and power would provide. Yes, some blessed day we shall indeed be the prettiest of all, for we shall be conformed to the image of His Son.

But our text in John 15 is not so much concerned with our election to salvation, as with our election to His service and to Christ-likeness. We are chosen here to bear fruit.

I am so glad it says that we have not chosen Him, but He has chosen us. If the choice had been mine, I might turn away from Him, or He might get disgusted with me and cast me off; but He has chosen me, knowing full well all that I was and ever would be, and so this gives me perfect assurance that He will never cast me out. I may grieve my Lord, but I can never disappoint Him, for He knew me long before He saved me, and chose me as His own.

He chose me, and He certainly knew He was not getting any bargain. He chose me, knowing what poor stuff I was. Almost anyone can do good work with excellent material and tools; but it takes a genius to do good work with poor stuff. Praise God, our blessed Lord is truly the genius. He did not choose me for what I was, but ever had in mind what He could do for me, in me and through me. Philippians 1:6 says that "He which hath begun a good work in you will perform (perfect) it until the day of Jesus Christ".

The fact that He chose me should keep me from pride on the one hand, and from an inferiority complex on the other. If He chose me, He has plans and purposes for me, and so I should yield myself unreservedly into His hands. Sometimes believers excuse themselves because they have so little talent, they claim. I heard a brother once bewail, in elaborate terms, his own insignificance, as he felt sorry for himself. Another brother, standing by, slapped him on the back, saying, "Don't be blue, brother. Remember that Noah had a jackass in the ark, too!"

He has chosen us because He has a place for us to fill. He

has ordained us. Every Christian is an ordained minister, according to our text; but don't get chesty, for that word "ordained" is simply the Greek word for "put". The subject here is fruitbearing, and a wise fruitgrower places his plants or trees where they will thrive the best. Even so, the Lord puts you and me here and there, to bear fruit for Him. He has chosen us for eternal glory, as 2 Timothy 2:10 shows; but He has also chosen us for present conformity to Christ and for present service (Rom. 8:29; Eph. 1:4; 1 Peter 2:9, etc.).

# Appropriation

*"Then came the soldiers, and brake the legs of the first, and of the other which was crucified with Him. But when they came to Jesus, and saw that He was dead already, they brake not His legs: but one of the soldiers with a spear pierced His side, and forthwith came there out blood and water. And he that saw it bare record, and his record is true: and he knoweth that he saith true, that ye might believe."*

(John 19:32-35)

I believe, as stated in my book on the Gospel of John, that John the apostle is recording a miracle in the above words. That's why he insists in verse 35 that he saw it happen, that what he says about it is true, and that he knows that what he says is true.

It is impossible for a stream of blood to flow from a dead body; hence, since it flowed from the body of our Lord after He had died, it bore witness to the fact that He was not an ordinary human being. In a sinner, the body goes to corruption immediately after the heart stops beating, but of our blessed Lord the psalmist said: "Thou wilt not suffer Thine Holy One to see corruption". Therefore, the blood flowing from the side of Christ does not attest His death (for we are plainly told that He was dead already), but it rather bears witness to who it is that died.

I believe that's the reason the apostle John is the only one of the writers of the four gospels who records this, because the theme of his gospel is who Christ is, while the synoptists call attention especially to what Jesus did. John tells us, in verses 30-31 of chapter 20, that "many other signs truly did Jesus in the presence of His disciples, which are not written in this book: But these are written, that ye might believe that Jesus is the Christ, the Son of God..." The chief purpose, John tells us here, was to call attention to who Jesus was - that He was the sinless Son of God. I am sure we all know that who a person is, is always of the most vital importance.

Many years ago, I was preaching in what was then Royal Palm Park in Miami, Florida. After I got through, a gentleman came up to me and handed me a card, announcing that he was giving infidel lectures in one of the city's theatres. Then he said, "I heard you say that the blood of Christ cleanses us from all sin. Now, that is nonsense. How many sins could a gallon of blood wash away? And besides, what difference is there between the blood of Christ and anybody else's blood? If you could take a vial filled with the blood of Christ and one filled with my blood, and take them to a chemist, you'd find that they both consisted of the same chemical elements."

Now, I had heard a good illustration some years before, and I tried it on this man. I held out to him a $10 bill and asked him whether he would like to have it.

"Well, yes, why not?" said he. "But," said I, "it is only a piece of paper with a picture on it. Why should an intelligent-looking gentleman like you want to bother with that?" "Because it's worth $10," said he. "No, I understand they print these things for something like a cent and a quarter a piece," said I. "I'll take it for $10, though," said the other. "But why?" I insisted. "Well, you know why. The

Government issues them and they are worth $10."

"Yes, that is certainly true," I replied. "Now, if *you* issued one of them, instead of its being worth $10, it probably would be worth ten years in jail for counterfeiting. The same $10 bill, you might be able to print it just as well as does the Government; but, nevertheless, if you print it, it would be a crime. If the Government prints it, it is currency.

"And that's your answer to your sneer at the blood of Christ. If you present your blood to God, He'll send you to hell for it. If you present the blood of Christ, He'll take you to heaven for it. It is not a question of the blood as such, but of whose blood it is. If Christ is God, then the price for the sinner's redemption has been paid. If He is not, then we have no Saviour. It all depends on who stands behind it. Praise God! Jesus, who shed His blood, is God, who poured forth His blood as man to die for the sins of sinful man."

One time, I saw a copy of a private cheque signed by John D. Rockefeller for $125,000,000. I believe at that time it was the largest cheque ever written by a private individual. That's nothing. I can write a cheque for that amount, too. I learned to write when I went to school. But if I did, you could throw it in the wastebasket; but when Rockefeller or Ford do it, it is worth every dollar it calls for. It all depends on "who" signs it.

Once a number of my friends sent me a cheque for $50.00 and, for the fun, eight men each wrote one word on the cheque. When my wife saw the cheque, she asked whether it was any good with all those different handwritings on it. "Yes, indeed, it is," I told her. The bank does not care who writes the cheque, only who signs it. With God, who Christ is, is what counts. "He that believeth Jesus is the Christ is born of God."

Have you appropriated Him as your own personal Saviour? Christ died on the Cross, but His death as such never saved a soul. At the Passover, the lamb was killed, but that did not save the firstborn from death. After that blood had been shed, each head of the house had to take that blood and apply it to the door of the house.

In spite of the fact that our blessed Lord shed His blood,

millions of souls have perished in their sins without Him. Have you said, like Paul, from your heart: "The Son of God loved me, and gave Himself for me?"

Years ago, I was walking with a brother in Philadelphia, when he pointed to a building and said to me, "Van, they put $85,000,000 in silver bars into that building yesterday. It's the Government Mint. They are going to convert them into silver currency." But, you know, his information left me completely cold. He had left out just two words which would have made a tremendous difference, and would have given me a real thrill. If he had said, "Van, they put $85,000,000 *for you* in that building", but he left those two words out. If he had even said, "They put $1,000,000 *for you* there", I might have managed to scrape along on that; but alas, he left me out altogether.

Everyone with a grain of sense knows the difference between a million dollars and a million dollars for you. That difference is small compared with the fact that Christ died and that He died *for you*. The fact that our blessed Lord shed His blood on the Cross to save sinners is wonderful beyond thought, but it means nothing to you until you personally accept Him as *your* Saviour. Do it now!

# Two Spiritual Attitudes

*"This spake He, signifying by what death he (Peter)
should glorify God. And when He had spoken this, He saith
unto him, Follow Me. Then Peter, turning about, seeth the
disciple whom Jesus loved following; which also leaned on
His breast at supper, and said, Lord, which is he that
betrayeth Thee?"*

(John 21: 19-20)

It appears to me that, in this incident, we have two kinds
of spiritual attitudes illustrated. Simon Peter was told to
follow the Lord; John followed without being told. How
often a similar effect is seen in christian experience.

Alas, there are believers who always seem to be like
Simon Peter here. They never do anything of their own
accord; they always have to be urged, encouraged, waited
on, nursemaided. This should not be so, for everyone who
knows and loves the Lord has the invisible urge within to
spur on in christian living and christian service, for "the love
of Christ constraineth us henceforth not to live unto
ourselves, but unto Him who died for us and rose again".

But, yet, there are believers who sulk when not asked or
recognized; who seldom or never do anything on their own
initiative. At times all of us need to be ashamed of our
spiritual sleepiness.

Some years ago, my wife said to me, "August, don't you
get weary sometimes? You preach to the Lord's people; you
seek to stir their hearts' affection for Christ; you weep for
them or thunder at them, and yet you see so little in the way
of results."

"Yes, that's true," said I after a pause for reflection. "But I
guess I operate pretty much the same as you do. You sweep
the house, dust the furniture, wash the dishes and make the

beds every day, and I don't see much in the way of results there, either. Now, just don't do the housekeeping for a month, and then you'll see results. So," said I, "I'll keep on ministering to the saints (myself included), and if I can only do my share to keep them from getting worse, I will be very successful, for that's all that you accomplish at home."

Yes, my fellow brothers and sisters, it just seems we need exhorting all the time; we're just failing humans at the best. If you are like John in our text, following without being told, I congratulate you. May the Lord bless you abundantly, and may you turn many a halting Peter into a fiery, fruitful follower of the Lord.

The secret for earnest devotion to Christ is found in that five-times-repeated statement concerning the apostle John as recorded in his Gospel, when he speaks of himself as "the disciple whom Jesus loved". A deep appreciation of the love of Christ to me will make the power of the love of Christ in me a mighty constraining force for good and a restraining power from evil.

# Alive and Showing It

*"The former treatise have I made, O Theophilus, of all that Jesus began both to do and teach...To whom also He shewed Himself alive after His passion by many infallible proofs, being seen of them forty days, and speaking of the things pertaining to the kingdom of God."*

(Acts 1:1, 3)

Note that the opening verse of the book of Acts speaks of an unfinished work. It speaks of that which Jesus began to do and teach.

On the Cross, He finished the work necessary for our redemption (see John 19:30 with John 17:4). Christ alone could meet the weighty problem of atonement for the sins of men. He alone could pay the price of sin, and He did so, praise His Name, when He died upon the Cross and rose in mighty power.

There He laid the foundation (1 Cor. 3:11) upon which the gigantic structure of Christianity was to be built. There He laid the foundation for the erection of His church. He thus began that work, which has been left to us to carry on. We could not redeem man by our death, but we can have a share in carrying the gospel of the grace of God everywhere, so that many may be saved and added to the church. This is the unfinished work referred to in Acts 1:1.

Note also that Jesus began to do before He taught. Of the Pharisees, He said that they "say and do not", but our blessed Lord ever practised what He preached. He set us an example so we might follow His steps, and we all know that example is much more potent than precept.

That's what the little fellow thought when his mother ordered him to bed: "Go up to bed, Johnny, it's time." And, to add emphasis to her words, she added, "The little chicks went to bed long ago". "Yes, I know," said the little sniper, "but the old hen went up first!" He believed in example before precept.

Note also the striking phrase in verse three that Jesus showed Himself to His disciples "alive". Why is that word "alive" there? He certainly could not have shown Himself if He had been dead. A dead person would have to be shown, but surely could not show himself. That "alive" seems very much like repetition; but we know it is there for a purpose, for God's Word is infinitely perfect.

As the Lord Jesus showed Himself alive physically after His physical resurrection, so we believers are to show ourselves alive spiritually after our spiritual resurrection from the death of sin (see John 5:24). And, while physically, of course, the Lord was alive, then, spiritually, we believers are both dead and alive, and can show ourselves either way. Do you remember that the Scripture teaches that we are both dead and alive at the same time? We are dead unto sin and alive unto God (Rom. 6:11). We are dead, yet our life is hid with Christ in God (Col. 3:3). Now we are to show ourselves alive unto God, as once we showed ourselves to be dead indeed, in trespasses and sins.

Now, when a believer lives a careless or sinful life, he is showing himself not alive, but dead. Then there is no evidence that he is a Christian, but rather the reverse. If God says we are dead, He wants us to be just that practically, not as follows:

I knew a dear old fisherman down south who told me this story. A man and his wife were very unhappy in their married state. This man was a sponge fisherman. On one of their trips, toward evening, he was washed overboard during a violent storm. His mates could not find him, so gave up the search, coming back to port some weeks later with the news that this man had drowned. Well, his wife did not care too much, and some months later became interested in another partner. The wedding date was set, but, to her consternation, on the evening before the scheduled ceremony, who should walk in the door but this drowned husband of hers! It developed that he had kept himself afloat all night, and a steamer on its way to the Orient had picked him up the next morning. Now, some four months later, he had found his way back home. His wife looked at him with disgust and blurted out: "You good-for-nothing thing! You're so ordinary that you can't even stay dead when you are dead!"

Well, that's the way it is when a believer yields to the lust of the flesh or spirit. God says he is dead, but he won't stay dead. He is not showing himself spiritually alive.

One way not to show oneself alive as a believer is to go to sleep. There are many warnings in the New Testament Scriptures against this sluggish habit. There is precious little apparent difference between a sleeping believer and a dead sinner.

A story has been told that, during the days of the P.W.A. or W.P.A., or whatever it was, a certain man died on the job, apparently from leaning too hard on a shovel, for he certainly had not been working. They sent for the coroner, and the joke ran the rounds that the coroner had to examine some thirty bodies before he found the dead man.

Sure enough, a sleeping Christian, lying down with dead sinners, looks no different than they. That's why God's Word bids the believer: "Awake, thou that sleepest, and arise from among the dead" (Eph. 5:14). If, out of a number of folks lying down together, it were impossible to tell whether they were dead or only sleeping, the moment one stood up, you'd know for sure he was alive at least.

Thus, an upstanding, outstanding Christian is showing himself alive. An "alive" Christian is a powerful testimony for Christ.

Two men walked into a taxidermist's store. While they were waiting for service, one began to criticize the exhibits. "Look at this parrot," he said after a bit. "You never saw a parrot holding his head in that peculiar fashion, or grasping its perch that way either, etc., etc." Just then the parrot spoke up and said, "Oh, is that so?" It happened to be a live parrot, and its aliveness immediately killed the criticism. So will an alive Christian.

We read in John 12:10-11 that the chief priests wanted to

put Lazarus to death, also, because by reason of him many of the Jews believed on Jesus. The very fact that Lazarus was alive was a powerful witness to the saving grace and power of Christ. The same will be true when you and I show ourselves alive, as Jesus did, by many infallible proofs. One of the best known of these proofs is given in our text: He spoke "of the things pertaining to the kingdom of God". Having believed, like Paul, we also speak. Let our mouths be filled with His praise all the day long, so that we may show ourselves truly spiritually alive!

# Salvation in Jesus' Name

*"Neither is there salvation in any other: for there is none other name under heaven given among men, whereby we must be saved."*

(Acts 4:12)

Three things are suggested in this text: (1) there is salvation; (2) salvation is not in any other; and (3) it is in the name of Jesus.

There is salvation. It does not say there was, nor yet that there shall be, but that there is. Right now there is salvation for any soul who will turn to God in repentance, and in saving faith to Christ.

It is not in any other, but in Jesus alone; not in the preacher or the priest, nor yourself, nor in your parents. Only Jesus saves. And this salvation, as the context shows, is only in the name of Jesus. Often there is wonderful magic in a name.

Years ago one of the popular slogans was "What's in a name?" In answer to this, a convict might be able to say, "There was pardon for me in the name of the governor who signed my reprieve". A businessman might say, "There was relief from disaster for me in the name of a friend who signed for me to help me out". And, praise God, the believer in Jesus says with exultant joy, "There is eternal salvation for me in the name of Jesus".

I remember so well, when I was but newly engaged in the work of the Lord, that someone sent me a cheque for fifty dollars - quite a sum to me in those days. I took the cheque to the local bank and the teller, an elderly man, looked at me over his glasses and said, "Is that your name on this cheque?" "Yes, it is." "Well, said he, "it will have to be endorsed by someone we know in this bank."

I knew better what endorse meant than a certain preacher I heard about. When he was told to endorse his cheque, he went to the counter and wrote on the back of the draft, "I heartily endorse this cheque", and presented it once more at the window. "No, no," said the teller, "not that way. We don't care to know what you think of this cheque. All we want is your signature on it."

So God does not care to know what you think of Christ. All He wants is for you to present your cheque at heaven's window with the name of Jesus on it.

I found, after some days, a christian businessman in that town who kindly scribbled his name on my cheque (and, believe me, it was a scribble), and when I presented it to the same teller again, he paid me out the fifty dollars without another word. There were fifty dollars for me in that man's name. There is salvation for any poor sinner in the name of Jesus. God will always honour that precious name.

Some folks have the idea that, when they stand before the throne of God in that day, they will get their cheques cashed on their own signature. But God, as it were, will look at them, as the bank teller looked at me, and say: "I'm sorry; we don't know you here. The only name we honour up here is the precious, availing name of Jesus." Get His name on your cheque and you can have anything you want, for, through Christ, all the riches of God's grace become yours. Have you experienced the power of the name of Jesus? "...Through His name whosoever believeth in Him shall receive remission of sins" (Acts 10:43).

# Warming Up

*"And when they were escaped, then they knew that the island was called Melita. And the barbarous people shewed us no little kindness: for they kindled a fire, and received us every one, because of the present rain, and because of the cold. And when Paul had gathered a bundle of sticks, and laid them on the fire, there came a viper out of the heat, and fastened on his hand...And he shook off the beast into the fire, and felt no harm."*

(Acts 28:1-3, 5)

We are in a cold world. There is great need for a fire to warm ourselves at, and others too. The Bible suggests a number of ways to warm ourselves, as follows:

1. We are to stir up the gift that is in us (2 Tim. 1:6). That verb "stir up" is used for poking the fire when it is dying down. A good way to do this is by taking a coal from the altar (Isaiah 6:6). In other words, to get back to the Cross and remind ourselves of all the matchless love displayed there. This is bound to set our cold hearts on fire afresh.

2. We must turn to the Word and meditate upon it, for, as Psalm 39:3 reminds us, "While I was musing, the fire burned".

3. We must be jealous for the honour of Christ, and see to it that we are true to Him and not carried away by false loves, as seen in 1 John 2:15. Jealousy for the honour of Christ is, as Songs 8:6 shows, like "coals of fire, which hath a most vehement flame".

4. Then there is the heat generated when saints meet together. As Ecclesiastes 4:11 says: "If two lie together, then they have heat: but how can one be warm alone?"

That's what the apostle Paul believed in, for he helped to make the fire burn more brightly by gathering a bunch of sticks to add them to the flame. Even so should you and I contribute our bit to keep the saints hot and on fire for God.

We cannot remain warm alone; we need the fellowship of saints.

A certain brother remained away from the meetings of the Lord's people and, of course, had plenty of reasons for his action - from his point of view. Everybody was at fault except himself. A godly fellow believer went to call on him. There happened to be a coal fire in the fireplace. So, after a few introductory remarks, the visitor took a white hot coal, with the tongs, out of the blaze and laid it on the hearth. After about ten minutes of desultory conversation, he got up, took the coal (by then cold and black) with his bare hand, threw it back into the fire, took up his hat and coat, said good-night and walked out without another word. The erring brother got the message alright. Get away from fellowship with other saints, and you'll soon get cold and dark.

Paul did not merely enjoy the heat, but he contributed to it. Some Christians come to enjoy the good things but never seem to think of doing anything themselves. As one brother said, he was once in an assembly which reminded him of one of those old English bedsteads - four brothers holding up the meeting and all the rest inside fast asleep.

When we go to sleep, the devil goes to sleep too, but when we get hot, the devil wakes up too. A snake woke up (I understand heat will rouse a snake out of its stupor; it will certainly wake the devil), and it bit Paul. Let believers wake up and the devil will wake up, too. He always goes after those who are awake and alert for Christ. And sometimes, alas, he is successful in harming them, even true Christians.

The barbarians looked for either one of two results - either for Paul to drop dead, or otherwise to swell up. Of course, spiritually speaking, a Christian cannot drop dead, for he is the possessor of life eternal; but a mere professing Christian can, as many a mere professing believer has been poisoned by Satan, to his everlasting doom.

But a Christian can swell up. Even the great apostle Paul could, and so he tells us there was given to him a thorn in the flesh, lest he should be exalted above measure, in other words, lest he should swell up (2 Cor. 12:7). But Paul did not swell either there or here.

I have known some believers whose service was largely spoiled by vanity. We are all in constant danger of this specially Satanic venom, injected by the originator of it, Satan (1 Tim. 3:6). Man is a curious creature: pat him on the back and often his head starts to swell.

Paul picked up a multitude of sticks. That is hard and humbling work, but very rewarding. It tells the story that we should contribute to the spiritual weal and zeal of God's people by way of hard and humble work, that thus they may be kept on fire for Christ and His name be glorified.

# Reactions to Sin

*"But now the righteousness of God without the law is manifested, being witnessed by the law and the prophets; Even the righteousness of God which is by faith of Jesus Christ unto all and upon all them that believe: for there is no difference: for all have sinned, and come short of the glory of God; being justified freely by His grace through the redemption that is in Christ Jesus."*

(Rom. 3:21-24)

Man has always been the same. From the Garden of Eden till now, human nature has not changed a bit. All have sinned and do come short of the glory of God. All alike need to be saved and can be saved in only one way - through the redemption that is in Christ Jesus, which becomes the possession of everyone who believes in Jesus.

That was true in the Old Testament, as well as in the New, though ostensibly the method of approach to God was different under law than it is now under grace. Yet, actually, approach to God always was only on the basis of faith in Christ, by which the righteousness of God was obtained (see verse 22 of our text).

Redemption through the blood of Christ was witnessed in the Old Testament by the law and the prophets (verse 21). The sacrifices of the law pointed on to the one all-sufficient sacrifice of Christ; and the prophets all spoke of the coming of Christ as the Saviour of sinners. See Isaiah 53:5-6 as an example.

I would like you to think with me of three ways in which the Jew, under law, would react in regard to the truth that man is a sinner and has come short of the glory of God.

The first type I can imagine is that one who, being aware of some specific sin, for instance, would say to himself: "So what? God does not mean anything to me. I know I'm a sinner; we're all sinners; what's so important about that? I'll just forget about the whole thing." That same class of folks exists today, for there are millions of souls who live their lives carelessly and thoughtlessly, very little concerned about the question of their sins and their responsibility towards God. They just forget about the whole thing. That attitude reminds me of an incident I remember from my childhood in Holland.

In our early years over there, we used only slates in school. They were very handy, could be used indefinitely (unless you broke them over some fellow pupil's head, which I must confess I did occasionally), and could be wiped off in a moment and thus be ready for the next subject. But in the higher grades, we graduated into the paper and ink class. I remember well the first morning this happened to me.

The teacher set us a writing lesson on the blackboard, which we were to copy. Not being used to a pen, I dipped the thing some three inches deep into the inkwell on my desk, and started off. Of course, the ink dripped off the pen onto the page, so I did what millions do when life's page is smirched and stained - I just turned over a new leaf, and started again. Some more ink dropped off and I turned over a few more new leaves.

After a while, things began to go a little smoother and I was about to congratulate myself, when I noticed my fingers were all dirty, too, with ink, and as I turned over the pages, the lower edge was all marked up. So, I wiped my fingers on my pants (as boys will do) and turned another page or two. But, alas, a last despairing drop of ink fell on this new beautifully white sheet of paper.

By this time, I began to get a little nervous and, forgetting I was not using a slate now, I spit on the page (as we used to do on the slate) and then tried to wipe the page clean with the sleeve of my jacket. What a mess this made! So, I rolled up the sleeve of my coat, turned over a couple of more pages and went at it once more. Now, at last, things began to look up and the lesson became transferred to my writing tablet.

Then, about 11:00 or 11:30, the teacher made the rounds of the room to see how we were getting on, and came eventually to my place. "Why, August," said she, "you're getting on famously! You are more than halfway through your pad already, the very first morning." And do you know what she did? All morning long, I had been turning the pages this way, but now she turned them back, one by one, that way; and as she turned the pages back, all the dirty mess came to light.

Even so will it be in the day when sinners shall be judged at the great white throne. God, as it were, will turn back the dark pages of the sinner's life, and the sins which he was glad to forget will be remembered, brought to light and punished.

Then, secondly, there would be the Jew in the Old Testament who was aware of his sin, and he would bring the offering prescribed by law - a bullock, or a sheep or a goat, or even two doves. He would hear the priest say to him that his sins were forgiven, and he would go home quite satisfied - perhaps shrug his shoulders and say to himself, "Well, that's that." But...were his sins truly forgiven? No, indeed. There was no real sense of guilt in his soul, no true repentance or conviction of sin. He just went through the motions, even as many religious folks go to church, perform some ritual, put their money in the collection, and go home, satisfied with a performance that not only did not put away their sins, but actually is obnoxious to God.

That type of attitude is described in Isaiah 1:10-13, for instance. God hates mere form without the spiritual reality. God does not look on the outside appearance, but on the heart.

Then there would be the third class: those who are truly aware of their guilt and, thoroughly repentant, would, in sincerity of heart and mind, bring their offering. Those who, like David, would realize that a "broken and a contrite heart, O God, Thou wilt not despise" (Psalm 51:17).

So, the only ones truly saved today are those who repent of their sins, come humbly to God, and trust for salvation in the all-availing sacrifice offered upon Calvary by God's Son, Jesus Christ our Lord. Those in the Old Testament were saved in view of the fact that Christ was going to die for them; we are saved because He did die for us.

# Law v. Grace

*"For sin shall not have dominion over you: for ye are not under the law, but under grace."*

(Romans 6:14)

Many illustrations could be used to show the contrast between law and grace. I would like to give you one from an experience my wife and I had some years ago which emphasized the fact that law drives, while grace leads. Law inspires fear and works on that principle, while grace inspires confidence. Law is, as it were, behind, pursuing the sinner; grace goes on ahead, leading the believer in the path of faith. This is what happened to us:

My wife and I entered a city in Virginia, where we were to

attend and speak at a conference of believers. We did not know the way to the home where we were to be entertained, but on the outskirts of the city we saw a traffic cop on a motorcycle, by the side of the road. So, I stopped and asked him whether he could direct us to this particular address. He thought a moment and then said: "Yes, I know where this is. It is quite a long way from here and, for strangers, rather hard to find, as it is just a short, two-block, dead-end street. I'll tell you what I'll do. I'll take you there."

We thanked him very much for his kind offer and started off right behind him. (It is the only police escort I'll probably ever have till the day of my funeral - if any, which I am not looking forward to, since I am a firm believer in the rapture of the saints. As has so often been said, we are not looking for the undertaker, but for the Uppertaker.)

Now, it so happened that the brother, at whose home we were to stay, passed us on his way home just as the police officer began to lead us. Everywhere this brother turned, the officer was close behind him, and we were behind the officer. When, at last, the brother drove into his short street, with the police still at his heels, he felt sure the law was really after him. He jumped out of his car, came running toward us, and stammered, "What's the matter, officer?" At that moment, he happened to see us, and his face broke out into a grin.

I thought of what a lovely picture this was of the difference between law and grace. To this brother, it was the law behind him, making him pretty uncomfortable; but, to us, it was grace in front of us. He got quite excited and worried; we were riding in high style and in supreme confidence. Nothing could happen to us (through grace, the law was on our side), for authority was being exercised on our behalf. Our friend was driving in fear; we were riding along in peace and triumph. That's what grace does for the believer. Love casts out all fear. Led by the Holy Spirit, the believer lives his life in calm assurance and peace, protected and guided all the way to his home in Glory.

# Self Life

*"For I know that in me (that is, in my flesh) dwelleth no good thing: for to will is present with me; but how to perform that which is good I find not."*

(Romans 7:18)

The seventh chapter of Romans is in sharp contrast to the eighth. Chapter 7 shows us man under law; chapter 8, under grace. In chapter 7, the dependence is on self; in chapter 8, on Christ. Chapter 7 is I, not Christ; chapter 8 is Christ and not I.

Look at this: *I, me* and *my* are found forty eight times in Romans 7, and only three times in Romans 8. Chapter 7 reminds me of an old ditty:

I had a little tea party
One afternoon at three;
'Twas very small, three guests in all:
Just I, myself and me.
Myself ate up the sandwiches,
While I drank up the tea;
'Twas also I who ate the pie
And passed the cake to me.

The natural man is just naturally an "I" specialist. Pride and self-importance come easily to human beings. On one occasion, a young lady said to her fiancé: "I read the other day that all very bright men are conceited." "Now," said he, "I don't know about that. I don't think I am conceited."

Paul wrote Romans 7 to set out in sharp juxtaposition the self-confidence of the natural man with the all-sufficiency of Christ our Saviour, as seen in Romans 8.

The patriarch Job also was afflicted with a bad dose of I-ism, as who isn't? In chapter 29, Job says *I, me* and *my* fifty two times. There he reminds me of a gentleman I once knew. As a friend and I were passing down the street, we saw this certain party going by on the opposite side of the road, and my friend said to me: "Van, if I could buy that man at my estimation of him, and sell him at his, I'd be a multimillionaire overnight!"

Yes, Job had a dose of it and it made him pretty miserable with his friends, who probably deserved it, but which did not justify Job. He said some very harsh things to them. Job was to learn that those aggravating friends of his did not put all that gall into Job, for it was already there. Our text says (and it included Job) that in our flesh dwells no good thing. All Zophar & Co. did was to bring all this out of Job. As a result, he was a better man and felt better when he got all that poison out of his system.

It is a wonderfully healthy lesson to learn that, by nature, we have nothing to be proud of - that in us, by nature, dwells no good thing. Only the grace of God can implant within us that which is good, divine life and a divine nature; and we learn that, when henceforth we live, it is not I, but Christ that liveth in me. Self is judged and set aside, and Christ takes the throne. That process is enlarged upon in Romans 8.

# Blessing in Christ

*"There is therefore now no condemnation to them which are in Christ Jesus, who walk not after the flesh, but after the Spirit."*

(Romans 8:1)

Paul, speaking for every believer, condemns himself repeatedly in Romans 7, but here, seen in Christ, he says there is no condemnation for the believer. There is no condemnation now, as our text states, nor ever, as John 5:24 assures us.

How completely the "I, me and my" of Romans 7 are obliterated in this very opening verse of chapter 8. We are said to be in Christ Jesus and, if any man be in Christ, he is a new creation (2 Cor. 5:17). Don't you see how this little, yet so big, word "in" wipes out self in one fell blow?

If I say there are a number of people in a certain room or building, I am not saying anything about them. They might be black or white, rich or poor, dead or alive, etc. I am making no distinction between good and bad, young or old, holy or vile. Even so, when a soul is saved and said to be in Christ, he himself is totally ignored and wiped off, as it were. The grace of God thus levels all - there is no difference for all have sinned (Rom. 3:23). "There is no difference...for the same Lord over all is rich unto all that call upon Him" (Rom. 10:12). In other words, the believer in Jesus is saved and blessed not because of who or what he is, but because of "where" he is - in Christ. Once it was I, not Christ; now it is Christ, not I.

I travelled for years by train, thousands of miles each year. To the best of my knowledge, no conductor ever asked me about my nationality as he came through the cars. He did not ask me whether I had been to college or not; whether I was a member of a church or was a heathen; whether I had bought my ticket, or if someone had given it to me, or whether I stole it. No, all he ever said was, "Your ticket, please."

If I had been a proud man, I might have felt offended by the way those officials ignored me personally. A passenger might have replied, when asked for his ticket, "Don't you know who I am? I'm the Archbishop of Chicago", and the conductor probably would have replied, "Glad to meet you, sir. Your ticket, please."

It is so with God. He does not care a rap who you are or who I am. He is no respecter of persons. All He is interested in is whether you have a ticket entitling you to His salvation, whether you are in Christ.

Noah's experience in the ark presents the same thought. It wasn't who Noah was that actually saved him from destruction, but where he was. The best possible person outside the ark was lost, while the worst sinner, if he had gone inside, would have been saved because, by faith, he had believed God. And it did not take long to get into the ark. "Only a step to Jesus; then why not take it now?"

In Christ, the believer is not only saved, but blessed. You remember the Passover night in Egypt? With the blood on the outside, the folks inside were having a feast beside the warmth, comfort and security of their firesides. In Christ there is salvation, sanctification and satisfaction; out of Christ there is danger, death and destruction.

# New Power Within

*"For the law of the Spirit of life in Christ Jesus hath made me free from the law of sin and death."*
(Romans 8:2)

This is the last we hear of "me" in Romans 8. We heard enough of the wretch in chapter 7; forty eight times there, and only three in this chapter. Christ, on the contrary, is mentioned only twice in chapter 7, and the Spirit not at all; but He is mentioned thirteen times in chapter 8, and the Holy Spirit eighteen times. That tells the story. It is *I* in Romans 7; it is *Christ* in Romans 8. That's why you hear a dirge of despair in chapter 7, and a note of triumph in chapter 8.

Safe and secure in Christ, the believer now lives by a new power resident within him, the rule of the Spirit of life in Christ Jesus.

On the wall of a Christian "Scientist" (so-called) Church in a city I know, this second verse of Romans 8 is carved; but, as the devil usually misquotes Scripture, so he did there. Three short words were left out: the words "the law of" in the latter part of verse 2, making the quotation read falsely like this: "for the law of the Spirit of life in Christ Jesus hath made me free from sin and death". Those poor deluded souls try to make themselves believe there is no sin and death, but God's Word refutes that nonsense. Sin and death are still here. They still affect the believer in Christ too, but they no longer rule in a believer's life. He is set free from the law (or the rule) of sin and death.

There is an almighty power indwelling the believer, the Holy Spirit of God, and He enables him to live a new life, setting him free from the dominion of sin.

We read in Romans 6:14, "for sin shall not have dominion over you: for ye are not under the law, but under grace".

Do you see that plane soaring through the sky? Why

doesn't it fall? Has the law of gravitation been suspended? Oh no, that plane is operating under a new law, the law of aviation, which enables it to defy the law of gravitation without defeating it. The law of aviation sets that plane free from the law of gravitation, and this is accomplished by the exertion of considerable power, generated by those big engines.

Even so, it takes power - divine, almighty power, the power of the Holy Spirit of God - to lift the believer off the earth into the realm of heavenly things, and to maintain him there in living touch with God. The earth and its things still have a strong gravitational pull, and unless the believer avails himself of the power of the Spirit, he is apt to come down to the level of the world with a thud.

As they used to say about the handling of a bicycle: "If you don't go on, you go off". But, praise the Lord, there is infinite power ever at hand to enable the Christian to live above the attractions and distractions of this evil world. "Set your mind on things above, where Christ sitteth at the right hand of God; not on things on the earth."

# Law Superseded

*"For what the law could not do, in that it was weak through the flesh, God sending His own Son in the likeness of sinful flesh, and for sin (or, rather, by a sacrifice for sin), condemned sin in the flesh."*

(Romans 8:3)

This verse assures us that sin has been totally condemned at the Cross, so that now we no longer are under the rule of law, which we could not keep, but under the rule of the Spirit, who keeps us.

Man was put under the law, and Paul tells us the law was holy and just and good; there was nothing whatsoever wrong with it. The reason it did not produce any good results is not because it was no good, but simply because man is no good. As our text says, "it was weak through the flesh".

Many years ago, a racket flourished for a time. Prominent newspapers carried this ad: "Sure cure for drunkenness! Guaranteed 100%! Will and can never fail! Send one dollar". Thousands responded and, in due time, got a nice card through the mail, something like a Christmas card, with a little powder sprinkled in it to make the bitter sweet. There were just two words embossed on the card: "Don't drink".

This, of course, was a perfect remedy for that dreadful affliction of drunkenness. It was foolproof, for it proved drunkards are fools indeed. It was alright, but it was weak through the flesh, for the poor souls were unable to carry out the advice.

The law, instead of curing the sinner, only demonstrated how sick he really was. It did its work in convicting the sinner of his sin and helplessness, and then the Lord Jesus came to provide the divine remedy for sin. The Cross is man's condemnation. It proves his total worthlessness in that it required God's Son to leave the glory to die for his sins. It condemns him that it might save him.

I was in a traffic court one day and heard a number of folks present plead guilty to minor infractions of the law. Each one was then fined a certain sum. Said I to myself: "How wonderfully different in God's court, for there everyone who pleads guilty is discharged. Christ has paid for our sins, and the guilty sinner is set free. Sin was condemned at the Cross, that the sinner who pleads guilty might not be condemned, but freely forgiven, for Christ's sake."

# Heirs of God

*"For ye have not received the spirit of bondage again to fear; but ye have received the Spirit of adoption, whereby we cry, Abba, Father. The Spirit itself beareth witness with our spirit, that we are the children of God: and if children, then heirs; heirs of God, and joint-heirs with Christ..."*
(Romans 8:15-17)

Grace is truly piled upon grace in this wonderful eighth chapter of Romans. First we were under condemnation, but then sheltered from that condemnation in Christ, indwelt by the Holy Spirit, given the place as sons in God's family, made heirs of God and joint-heirs with Christ.

The New Testament is our Lord's last will and testament where, through His death, He has made us the beneficiaries of all His vast wealth. Not only did our Lord make His will, and then died to make it valid, but He rose again to see to it that our property becomes truly ours. We shall enjoy our riches forever in the company of, and in perfect fellowship with Him, for we are joint-heirs with Christ.

Are you an heir of His vast wealth, of the unsearchable riches of Christ? The title to it can be obtained simply, for our text says, "if children, then heirs." We become the children of God by faith in Christ Jesus (Gal. 3:26) and, as a result, we automatically become His heirs.

Shortly after the famous Andrew Carnegie died, a newspaper cartoon showed a tramp leaning against a lamppost, crying. A policeman passing by said to him: "What are you sobbing about?" "Why, haven't you heard?" replied the hobo. "Andrew Carnegie died last night and left about 500 million dollars." "Well, what's that to you?" asked the officer. "What are you crying about? He wasn't no relative of yours, was he?" "No," said the tramp, "that's what I'm crying about."

It is too sad that so few are anxious to share in the eternal grace and glory of Christ, which is available on such simple terms.

# Groans and Waits

*"For I reckon that the sufferings of this present time are not worthy to be compared with the glory which shall be revealed in us. For the earnest expectation of the creature* (each time in this passage the word should be creation rather than creature) *waiteth for the manifestation of the sons of God.*

*"For the creation was made subject to vanity, not willingly, but by reason of Him who hath subjected the same in hope, because the creation itself also shall be delivered from the bondage of corruption into the glorious liberty of the children of God.*

*"For we know that the whole creation groaneth and travaileth in pain together until now. And not only they, but ourselves also, which have the firstfruits of the Spirit, even we ourselves groan within ourselves, waiting for the adoption, to wit, the redemption of our body.*

*"For we are saved by hope: but hope that is seen is not hope: for what a man seeth, why doth he yet hope for? But if we hope for that we see not, then do we with patience wait for it.*

*"Likewise the Spirit also helpeth our infirmities: for we know not what we should pray for as we ought: but the Spirit itself maketh intercession for us with groanings which cannot be uttered."*

(Romans 8:18-26)

This portion deals with groans and waits. Each is mentioned three times. The groans have to do with the present; the waits bid us to look on to the bright future that beckons the believer onward and upward.

The whole creation groans - verse 22; the believer groans - verse 23; the Spirit within groans - verse 26. Thus, there are groanings that are uttered (v. 22); groanings that should not be uttered (v. 23); and groanings that cannot be uttered

(v. 26).

I believe every thinking person will agree that this world is full of groans, of pain and suffering. Verse 20 tells us that Adam is the responsible party for the trouble in the world, as also says Romans 5:12, for by one man sin entered into the world, with all its dreadful resulting consequences. As far as man is concerned, there is no hope. The hope with which verse 20 closes is not due to the first Adam, but to the last, to our Lord Jesus Christ.

Verse 19 well says that the earnest expectation of all creation waits for the manifestation of the sons of God. That manifestation takes place when Christ comes to take sinners out and bring millennial blessing into this world. Colossians 3:4 tells us that the sons of God shall be manifested when Christ is manifested at His public second coming, of which almost all the Old Testament prophets spoke so glowingly. The only hope for this poor world is the return of Christ, our Saviour. Then, as verse 21 says, creation shall be delivered from the bondage of corruption into the liberty of the glory of the children of God. Not the glorious liberty, as in the King James version, but the liberty of the glory. Glorious liberty would refer to the kind of liberty, but the liberty of the glory refers to the time of liberty.

This is the day of grace. The day of glory comes when Jesus comes back. Then the world shall be delivered from the ravages of sin. We believers wait for that, too. However, we already now enjoy a definite liberty, but it is the liberty of grace, for Scripture tells us that our souls have been set free from sin, though, as to our bodies, we must wait till the coming of Christ to take us home. We are urged now to stand fast in the liberty wherewith Christ has made us free (Gal. 5:1).

That liberty, of course, the inanimate or animate (plant and animal life) knows nothing about. Only the saint, redeemed, liberated by the death of Christ, experiences this. Yet, in a certain indirect way, even vegetables, animals, yea and sinners around us, do enjoy a little of this liberty of grace that the believer rejoices in.

A certain huckster years ago got brightly saved by God's

grace. He had been a beast of a man, a drunkard, vile with his mouth, and cruel to his horse that drew his fruit-and-vegetable cart. But now there was a wonderful change in his life, and all men did marvel.

Then, one day, giving his testimony as to what Christ had done for and in him, he told his hearers: "Everybody on my route knows I am saved. They know it by the life I live; they know it because I am so happy in Jesus; they know it because I talk to them about my blessed Saviour. Yes," he went on as he waxed more enthusiastic by the minute, "even my horse knows I am converted. Every once in a while, my horse turns its head around and looks at me and says, 'What on earth has happened to you? You used to treat me so cruelly, and now you are so gentle and kind. I don't get it; what gives?' You see," he concluded, "even my horse knows I am saved."

And so it is. Everyone and everything around is affected by the presence of believers in Jesus. They shed an influence abroad which is felt, in spite of whether men believe in Christ or not. Christianity is a mighty force for good in this wicked world. When believers are taken out when Jesus comes, fearful moral and spiritual catastrophes will sweep over this sinful scene.

In the meantime, the whole creation groans, and we believers are not exempt, for verse 23 states that we ourselves, who have the firstfruits of the Spirit, groan within ourselves while we wait for the redemption of our body. Our bodies are subject to the same ills, accidents and deaths as the bodies of all men, so we feel the weight of things down here as much, yea more, than sinners do. But let us note carefully two words in this verse 23.

Once upon a time, I visited a dear sister in Christ who was pretty much distressed, and for a couple of hours she poured out all her troubles into my ears. When she finally stopped, and I got a chance to break in on the torrent, I said to her: "Dear sister, you have, for quite a while, told me all your troubles and cares, and you have said almost nothing about your Lord and His many blessings. Do you think that's right?" "Why, yes," she said, "doesn't the Bible say that even we Christians groan, too, while waiting for the redemption of our bodies?" "Yes, that's true," I replied, "but you should have quoted the whole verse. You left out two little words. That passage says that we believers groan 'within ourselves', but you have been blubbering it out now for two hours."

You see, dear believer, there is so much crying, cursing, weeping, and blaspheming coming constantly from the lips of men, that the Lord does not want us to add to that doleful dirge. He delights to hear our praises instead of our groans. We must do our groaning silently, and our singing, shouting and praising Him aloud. I think the Lord must be pleased when, from this sad world, He hears the sweet strains of praise and adoration ascend to His throne. Let's see to it that He gets more of that from us from now on. While we wait, let us pray and serve and sing!

# Assurance

*"Blessed be God, even the Father of our Lord Jesus Christ, the Father of mercies, and the God of all comfort."*
(2 Cor. 1:3)

We are usually very much concerned with our physical comfort, but God is interested much more in our spiritual comfort. God is the God of all comfort, according to this text, though this does not refer to bodily ease but, rather, to peace of soul.

In going through the Scriptures with the concordance, I discovered that, in the Bible, comfort practically never has a physical connotation, but always has in view the welfare of the soul.

When we welcome a visitor into our homes, we point him, perhaps, to the best chair in the room and say, "Sit down; make yourself comfortable." Yet that person, while physically comfortable, might be very, very unhappy and restless indeed in soul.

A man well off financially, we say, is comfortably fixed; but real comfort is only found in the enjoyment of the riches of God's grace - riches that do not take wings to themselves and fly away. Yes, man thinks of his physical state and forgets the far more vital unseen realities that are eternal.

Many years ago, I was in the jail at Muskegon, Michigan, as a visitor, I'm glad to say. I gave a tract to one of the inmates, but he shoved it back at me and said, "I don't want it." "Why not?" I asked. "I'm not a goat," said he, "I don't eat paper!" "But I did not give this to you to eat; I gave it to you to read," I replied. "Yes, I know, but I want something to eat. They starve you to death in this jail. They give you what they call two meals a day. Meals? Bah! I want something to eat," he complained. "What for?" said I to him. He retorted, "What for? Well, a fellow's got to eat, doesn't he?" I answered, "Not that I know anything about; it isn't at all necessary."

"But if you don't eat, you'll die," said he. I replied, "Well, that's alright. What difference does it make whether you live or die? Do you think the world can't get along without you? Do you think that many people will care the slightest one way or the other? Do you think the President of the United States will lose a night's sleep if you should die? It's of no importance at all whether you live or die; but what is important is where you are going after you are dead, for you are going either to heaven or to hell. That's why I gave you the tract, because it points the way to Christ so that you might be saved from your sins and escape the eternal jail of the lake of fire, and be blessed by God's wonderful grace."

And then I told him that when I talked to him in that startling fashion, I was following the truth spoken by the lips of the Lord Jesus Christ Himself. I turned him to John 6:27, where the Lord Jesus told His hearers: "Labour not for the meat which perisheth, but for that meat which endureth unto everlasting life." The Lord did not say, "Don't work too much," or, "Work first for food to put into your body," but, "Don't labour for that at all." He told His audience that no one ought to pay the least attention to the needs of his body till his soul was saved.

Be sure, then, that your soul is comfortable, for if you don't, like the rich man in hell in Luke 16, you may be eternally uncomfortable in the flame of God's judgment. And this comfort is not merely solace or consolation; nay, the word means "one who stands by you in time of trouble and need".

First, He is there to save your soul; then, to sustain and strengthen you in every hour of trial and sorrow. Thus, experiencing God's comfort for yourself, you will be able to comfort others with the comfort wherewith you yourself were comforted of God.

# Life - a Sweet Savour

*"Furthermore, when I came to Troas to preach Christ's gospel, and a door was opened unto me of the Lord, I had no rest in my spirit, because I found not Titus my brother: but taking my leave of them, I went from thence into Macedonia. Now thanks be unto God, which always causeth us to triumph in Christ, and maketh manifest the savour of His knowledge by us in every place.*

*"For we are unto God a sweet savour of Christ, in them that are saved, and in them that perish: to the one we are the savour of death unto death; and to the other the savour of life unto life. And who is sufficient for these things? For we are not as many, which corrupt the Word of God: but as of sincerity, but as of God, in the sight of God speak we in Christ."*

(2 Cor. 2:12-17)

I have often been thankful for the example of godly living and devoted service set before us in the Scriptures in the life of the apostle Paul. If we only had the Lord Jesus as our example to imitate (see 1 Peter 2:21), we might feel how utterly impossible it would be for us to approximate that perfect standard. But when we see that marvellous life lived by a human being who was subject to all the failures, and affected by all the passions man is heir to, we take courage.

Paul often passed through times of anxiety, disappointments, and even lack of faith. As he says in 2 Corinthians 7:5: "We were troubled on every side; without were fightings, within were fears." But one thing he never did - he never complained, and that is quite a lesson for us to profit by. Grumbling and complaining come so easily to most of us.

Once two men met on the street and, after the usual greetings and inquiries as to business, sports, etc., one said: "And how is your wife?" "Oh," said the other, "she can't complain." His friend sadly shook his head and replied: "My, my, is she that bad?"

Like all the great men of the Bible, and even like our blessed Lord Himself, Paul often wept (see 2 Cor. 2:4; Acts 20:19, 31, etc.). He never wept for himself, but always for others. The sorrows and burdens he carried were borne for the saints he loved so much. He had the care of all the churches. Personally, he always rejoiced in the Lord, as he intimates in 2 Corinthians 6:10: "sorrowful, yet alway rejoicing".

Our Lord often wept, and on one occasion wept for Himself, in the garden of Gethsemane, when with strong crying and tears, His soul felt, to its utmost depths in anticipation, the awful horror of the Cross (Heb. 5:7). But, praise God, since neither Paul, nor you nor I shall ever know the judgment of God, the one reason justifying us to weep for our own troubles is removed.

I once stayed in a home where, some years before, the only son of the family had been taken away by death rather suddenly. He was a bright, happy young Christian, and his homegoing was a triumphant one. Yet, five years later, the mother had never touched anything in his bedroom, and would not let anyone sleep in it. She had built a little bench at the graveside, and every good day she would sit there, look at the grave and weep.

I think I spoke as roughly to that christian mother as I ever did in my life. I tried to show her that her neighbours must have gotten the impression that to go to heaven was about the worst tragedy that could happen to anyone. "You are not weeping for him," said I, "but for yourself. You are shedding tears over a loved one gone to heaven, and you are dry-eyed over sinners going to hell." It was not so with Paul, or Joseph in Egypt, or our blessed Lord.

In our text, after expressing his anxiety, all of a sudden Paul bursts forth into a paean of praise, saying: "Thanks be unto God, who always causeth us to triumph in Christ." Here, as the apostle so often does in his writings, he employs a military figure so well known in those days. He sees himself marching on in a mighty triumphal procession, like those staged by the Roman conquerors of those stirring days when they came home after some signal victory. Such parades were called "triumphs", and for them a triumphal arch was built at the entrance to the city.

Paul sees himself, not under the leadership of a Roman emperor, but marching on under the victory banner of the greatest Victor of all time, the Son of God and Saviour of men. From the discouraging things around, he lifts the eye of faith heavenward and, by faith, sees himself led victoriously (and all the saints, as well) under the banner of Christ, the Captain of our salvation.

He not only sees himself as a captive of matchless love, but sees some of the preciousness of Christ put upon him, for he says, "We are unto God a sweet savour of Christ; a savour which we are to spread about us, so that to precious dying souls it may become a savour of life unto life." How wonderful that, to put it bluntly, when God smells the believer, He smells the same sweet fragrance as He does in His beloved Son.

This is illustrated in John 12, when Mary anointed the Lord and then wiped it off with her hair. Everywhere Mary went, and everywhere Jesus went, the same sweet odour was manifest, and probably some of its sweet fragrance was also experienced by those nearby.

Considering the immense responsibility of making the preciousness of Christ known to those about us, Paul asks the question: "And who is sufficient for these things?" And then replies: "We are not as many which corrupt the Word of God."

Dr. A. T. Robertson, the famous Greek scholar, says that the verb employed in this answer of Paul's suggests the habit of hucksters to put the best fruit on top. Paul says he is not like that. You know, of course, how hucksters operate. When you buy a quart of strawberries, they have twenty five beautifully big ones on top, five each way. But if you are naive enough to think they are all that nice underneath, you haven't lived very long yet. Underneath are the small ones, the spoiled ones, or the half-ripe ones, etc.

The huckster does put the best fruit on top, but Paul says

he does not, when it comes to telling forth the grace and glory of Christ. Why doesn't he? For a very simple reason; because it is impossible. No matter what the human tongue might try to say about our wonderful Lord, it would fall utterly short of the reality. No heart can conceive, no tongue can possibly tell, His glorious worth. In fact, we don't even know much yet, for at present we know only in part. With the Queen of Sheba, we'll say when we see Him: "The half was never told us."

# Three Epistles

*"Do we begin again to commend ourselves? Or need we, as some others, epistles of commendation to you, or letters of commendation from you? Ye are our epistle written in our hearts, known and read of all men: forasmuch as ye are manifestly declared to be the epistle of Christ ministered by us, written not with ink, but with the Spirit of the living God; not in tables of stone, but in fleshy tables of the heart."*

(2 Cor. 3:1-3)

The emphasis in the first verse is, I believe, on that word "again". It suggests that Paul had commended himself to the Corinthians before, and now he wants to know if this needs to be repeated. He commended himself wherever he went in at least a twofold way: (1) by the message he preached, which proved to be the power of God to the saving of souls and transforming of lives, and (2) by his own holy, devoted life; in other words, by his lips and by his life.

But false teachers had come in, drawing the hearts of the Corinthian saints away from this servant of Christ, as Paul tells them in other places in his epistles to them.

The same thing may be said in relation to our blessed Lord Himself. He, too, commended Himself to us by His holy life and by His words of grace and truth. Paul commended himself to the Corinthians, but God commends His love to us, in that, while we were yet sinners, Christ died for us. Our hearts grow cold toward our Lord, as the hearts of the Corinthians did towards Paul.

And so, throughout the New Testament epistles, there is a repeated re-commendation of Christ's love to us. (2 Corinthians 11:1-3 deals with that thought.) Paul asks and, in intent, answers the questions: "Do I need either to be commended to you, or by you?" Of course not! Neither does the Lord Jesus. But let me say that, while the Lord graciously delights in having true believers commend Him to others, He certainly does not want the commendation of unbelievers. God does not care to know what the sinner thinks of Christ. He does not want his approval of Christ. He wants the sinner's acceptance of Christ.

Paul, replying to his own question, goes on to say: "Ye are our epistles, written in our hearts." He then continues and speaks of three letters in these three verses which are worth considering; and I would like you to look at them in the sense that the same things Paul says here concerning himself, are true in relation to the Lord Jesus and our attitude towards Him.

In verse 2 we are seen written in the heart of Christ; in verse 3 Christ is written in our heart; and, at the close of verse 2, we are a letter which men read. Men cannot see me written in the heart of Christ. They cannot see Christ written in my heart; but they can see me and my life, in which Christ should be translated into practical living, as Paul says: "To me to live is Christ."

First of all, then, we are written in the heart of Christ. That way, we can nevermore be erased. It means that we are eternally secure. In the Old Testament, the high priest wore a breastplate with twelve jewels on it on which were engraved the names of the twelve tribes of Israel, suggesting in this way that the people of God were on the heart of the high priest. But, being only on his heart, on the outside, he could take, and did take, them off at times.

But, since we are written in the heart of Christ, we simply can't be lost. We are always there, precious to Him. Nothing is able to separate us from the love of God which is in Christ Jesus our Lord. There is truly a great difference between the outside and the inside.

Years ago, when we first came from the Bahamas to the States, we drove up north from Florida in an old jalopy. Our children had never seen trains, and were much interested in them. One day our oldest son, Elliot, said to me: "Daddy, that man who steers the train must be good. I don't see how he manages to keep all those cars on those narrow rails. Boy, he knows how to steer!"

So, when we came to a siding with some freight cars on it, I stopped our buggy, and my boy and I crawled underneath one of those freight cars. I showed him the flanges on the wheels and explained to him how those kept the cars from getting off the track - that it was not due to the skill of the engineer. When he looked at the outside of the cars, he wondered how they stayed on the tracks, but when he looked on the inside, he wondered how they could come off. Praise God, so it is in the spiritual life. Get a look by faith at the inside of the heart of God, and you'll see how blessedly secure you are.

Next, Christ is written in our heart, according to verse 3. Not with ink, but with the Spirit of God, written in fleshly tables of the heart. Ordinarily, the heart of man is like stone, as we read in Ezekiel 11:19, where God says: "I will take the stony heart out of their flesh, and will give them an heart of flesh." That's what our text is talking about.

The fleshly table of the heart is the heart of one who has been saved by the grace of God, and in whom God has substituted his heart of stone for a heart of flesh that readily takes impressions of God's Word and mind.

Normally the heart of a child is soft and tender and that is the time to win it for Christ, for as the years accumulate, the heart often grows hard and unresponsive as a stone; hardened, as Hebrews 3:13 says, through the deceitfulness of sin.

I have sometimes asked children in Sunday School why it is that I see the paws of a cat or a dog in the concrete of the sidewalk, while I, who weigh 200 pounds, do not leave the marks of my paws there when I walk over it. They all know the answer, of course. The dog or cat walked on it when the cement was soft.

There isn't much hope for softness in the case of hard concrete; it's too late for that, but, praise God, not so in the case of sinners. Upon conversion, God takes the stony heart out and puts within, so to speak, a heart soft and tender, able and ready to take impressions, upon which the Spirit of God writes a letter all about the Lord Jesus Christ. Every time a Christian reads the Word of God or hears it spoken, the Spirit writes a letter of Christ upon the heart. Not a word of it is ever lost.

I so often hear complaints from saints that they have such a poor memory, and they just can't remember anything at all, and that the preaching of the Word does them so little good. And I tell them: "Bless you, dear sister or brother, God is not writing on your mind, according to our text, but on your heart."

One dear lady told me years ago: "Oh my, I have a memory like a sieve; I just can't remember anything at all." I looked at her with my mouth wide open and said: "Ma'am, if I could have a memory like a sieve, I'd thank God for it upon my knees three times a day. The trouble with me is the other way. You know, a sieve is one of those contraptions that lets all the little things through and holds the big things. My mind's just the other way. I can remember all the trifles. I believe I remember every joke I hear, but worthwhile things slip my mind most of the time." Oh, for a memory like a sieve!

But don't let me get away from my contention. It isn't the mind that counts; it is the heart. I am written in His heart for security and blessing; He is written in my heart for spiritual power and enjoyment, to be expressed in responsive worship and service.

Now, no outsider can read these two letters, for they are

both internal. But outsiders should see and read Christ in us, so we must translate these internal letters into visibility, and that is suggested in the latter part of the second verse of our text. We are to be a letter "known and read of all men".

The world does not read the Bible or understand it when read, so we must translate it into understandable language in the lives we live. People read us, and so Christ should be magnified in our bodies. We must live in communion with Him and must exhibit the life of Christ to the world about us.

As has been said, the exports must keep pace with the imports. The auditor of today must be the orator of tomorrow. It is easier to talk than to walk.

I read once of two horses pulling a heavily laden wagon up a steep hill. The wheels had not been greased for a long time, and the whole rig groaned terribly. At last the horses stopped, turned around to look at the wagon and said: "Oh, shut up! You're not doing the work; we are!" The thunder makes the noise and takes the credit, but it is the lightning that does the work.

A man living in the country got the bright idea of rigging up a doorbell by means of some dry-cell batteries, wire, etc., and it worked like a charm. So, he decided he might as well fix himself an electric light, too, over his bed. He got some more batteries and the other necessary paraphernalia, but the thing did not work. So, he told his woes to an electrician, who replied scornfully: "You sap, don't you know any better? Don't you know it takes a lot more power to give light than to make noise?"

That's the way it is in the spiritual realm, too. Talking is sometimes very easy, but to live a life honouring the Lord Jesus is harder, for the reason that, when living a truly christian life, one meets with opposition. The reason it takes more power to give light than to make noise is that there is a filament in the light bulb, made of material that resists electric current. When someone resists you, you know how easily you get hot, too, don't you? It's that way in the bulb; it is the resistance that creates the glow and produces the light.

Let's not forget these three epistles. We are written in Christ's heart; He is written in ours; and He Himself is seen written in our lives - Christ known and read of all men (see Gal. 2:20).

# Christ's Poverty

*"For ye know the grace of our Lord Jesus Christ, that, though He was rich, yet for your sakes He became poor, that ye through His poverty might be rich."*

(2 Cor. 8:9)

In a beautiful setting, we see this magnificent jewel mounted for our admiration, adoration and imitation. In this chapter, which deals with the subject of christian giving, our eyes are focused upon Him who is, at once, the greatest Gift and the greatest Giver, as well. Let us feast our souls on this exquisite beauty of grace and glory!

At the outset, this precious verse tells us that He who gave Himself was none other than the eternal God, for we are told that He was rich and became poor. Now, it is quite evident that Christ was never rich down here; therefore, if He was rich, He must have lived ere He came to earth. And so it is, praise His Name! He was rich in heaven; rich in God the Father's complacent love; rich in the worship, acclaim and service of millions of angels. In infinite grace, He left that glory to become poor. He is the only one who ever came from heaven to live upon earth as man.

A little boy once asked his mother whether babies come from heaven. Her unwise reply was, "Why, sure, they do!" He replied, "No wonder then, Mother, that they put our new baby out. He's crying all the time. They didn't want him in heaven."

But, of course, the mother was wrong. Babies start here. The only one who ever came from heaven was the Babe laid in Bethlehem's manger.

Our Lord is the only being with the right and the opportunity to choose the home and the family into which He wanted to be born. With us, this is entirely a matter of accident, as far as we are concerned. We have no choice as to our parents, and they, poor souls, have to put up with what they get.

Our Lord could have chosen to come into the home of the ultra rich and great; but He saw fit to make His entry into this world in a home of poverty and humility. In that way, even the lowliest would feel free to approach Him.

However, our Lord was not really poor when it comes to material things. Even down here, all the resources of the eternal God were at His disposal. He could feed thousands with five little buns. I would not consider myself poor if I could make food whenever I wanted to. I wouldn't need the supermarket.

When the Lord wanted money on one occasion, He sent Simon Peter to the lakeside to get it out of the mouth of a fish. I could not consider myself poor if I could go and get money any time I felt like it. Of course, our Lord never did things like that for His own needs, but only to supply the needs of others. He came not to be ministered unto, but to minister.

No, the poverty of our verse, which Jesus knew, was not poverty in a material way. The fact that Christ was born in a stable and that He never owned anything in His life does not make us rich. Neither material poverty nor riches are in view in our text. The poverty of 2 Corinthians 8:9 is the spiritual poverty our Saviour knew, and the riches are the spiritual, unsearchable riches of Christ, which are ours by faith in Him. The poverty of our verse is the fearful spiritual poverty our Saviour knew when He hung on Calvary's bitter Cross. It is through that redemptive sacrifice that we are made rich indeed.

Yes, that's where Christ was poor. There His disciples all forsook Him and fled, for He looked for some to take pity and there were none, and for comforters and He found none. There, too, He was stripped of all His assets, shamed, dishonoured and numbered with transgressors. A person who has no friends and no assets is poor indeed, but this is not yet the real poverty our Saviour knew.

Not only was He robbed of all His rights and possessions, but He was loaded down with all the liabilities of ages, with all our sin and guilt. He took upon Himself all the debts of ages. He, who knew no sin, was made sin for us. A person is truly poor who has no friends to stand by him, no assets and nothing but liabilities; and our blessed Lord was in that condition upon the Cross of Calvary.

But that still is not the full poverty of our text. Many others have been in a minor predicament like that, but could still turn, in all their desperate need, to God and find solace there. But oh, when Jesus turned to God, He found His face turned away from Him in those hours of awful darkness, and we hear Him cry: "My God, My God, why hast Thou forsaken Me?" That, dear reader, is the supreme poverty of our text. It is through that fearful suffering of Jesus Christ our Lord that we are made rich, blessed with all spiritual blessings in the heavenlies in Christ.

Do you know anything about this grace of Jesus Christ? Note that it says "the grace of our Lord Jesus Christ", which means the grace seen in the life of Christ. It does not say the grace of God. The grace of God points to grace at its source; the grace of the Lord Jesus Christ points to the grace in its course - in the channel through which it comes to us.

The grace of God, we read in Titus 2:11-12, teaches us to deny ungodliness and worldly lusts. In other words, it teaches us to say "No" to evil in our lives; but the grace of the Lord Jesus Christ is seen in the fact that He denied Himself all that is good, and it is presented in our text as an example for us to imitate.

Christ had no sin. He could not, and did not need to, deny Himself things that are evil, but we do, because we are still capable of sinning. The grace of the Lord Jesus Christ is seen in that He denied Himself all that was good in itself in order that He might be able to bless and save us.

He denied Himself the glories of heaven, and became a stranger away from home for over thirty three years. It led Him to deny Himself the worship and service of angels in the glory above, and to live a life of lowliness and humility, often misunderstood even by His own disciples, and hated and persecuted by His enemies.

It is that example that we are to follow. As He became poor that we might be rich, so we are to deny ourselves, that others, through our poverty, may be blessed.

A boy once told his mother that he wanted to send some money to the mission work. His mother said that would be nice, but it would have to be the fruit of self-denial. He would have to go without something or other, and give that money thus saved to the cause. For instance, she told him: "How about giving up candy? That would amount to perhaps fifty cents a week, and you could give that to the Lord's work." That was alright with the boy. But a few hours later, he came back to her and said: "Mother, does it have to be candy that I give up?" She replied, "Well, no, not necessarily. What else would you be thinking of?" Said he: "How about giving up soap?" It's like our giving; often, it does not cost us too much.

A little girl confided to her mother that she was giving her daddy a pair of slippers for his birthday. "That's fine," said her mother, "but where are you going to get the money?" "Why," said the little miss, with her eyes wide open at such an ignorant question, "Daddy is going to give it to me!" But don't laugh! All we ever give to the Lord is what He has first given to us.

# God's Unspeakable Gift

*"Thanks be unto God for His unspeakable gift."*
(2 Cor. 9:15)

Perhaps the simplest illustration of the blessedness of the gospel of God's grace is to tell people that it is the gift of God. The gift of God is eternal life, through Jesus Christ our Lord. Everyone knows what a gift is and what one has to do to own it. While a gift does not cost the recipient anything at all, it may cost the giver a considerable sum of money. It usually has to be bought and paid for. Even so our blessed Lord paid for the gift of eternal life with His own precious blood. As we sometimes sing: "Jesus paid it all; all to Him I owe."

That's why Romans 6:23 says, "...the gift of God is eternal life through Jesus Christ our Lord". It has to come through someone; someone must be the giver. And all one has to do in accepting a gift is to say, "Thank you". So says Paul in our text: "Thanks be unto God for His unspeakable gift."

Whether that gift has reference to our Lord Jesus Himself ("for God so loved the world that He gave His only begotten Son"); or whether it refers to the great gift of eternal life which is ours by faith, for that, too, is the gift of God; in either case, we owe Him thanks that we find it impossible to express, for the gift that is itself unspeakable. The gift is called unspeakable, its immensity passes all possibility of telling. God bestows numberless gifts upon us, but none comparable with this greatest of all gifts; His Son, and eternal life in Him.

Years ago, a Christian stood on a street corner in a big city. It was almost Christmas time, cold, with a thick covering of snow. While he waited for a streetcar, a newsboy approached him and asked if he wanted to buy a paper. "No," said he, "I don't have any special need for a paper right now." Then, looking at the boy, he noticed that he was blue from the cold, for he was but thinly clad, with his bare feet in old torn shoes.

He said to the lad: "You ought not to be out in this weather and at this time of night. Why don't you go home and get warm?" "But I've got to sell papers," said he, "I've got to help my mother to care for the rest of the family." So the Christian put his hand in his pocket, took out a handful of change and said: "Here, help yourself to a piece of money out of my hand, and go into this cafe, and at least get yourself a cup of hot coffee to warm yourself a little."

The boy took a nickel out of the man's hand, and then, before going off, said: "Did you say a nickel, mister?" "No," was the reply, "I said you could have a piece of money - just one piece." So, the kid dropped the nickel and spied a dime. "Can I have the dime, mister?" "Yes, I told you that you could have one piece."

Then the lad spied a quarter, dropped the dime, and, looking again, noticed a half dollar. "Say, mister, can I have the half dollar? Can I?" The man answered, "Yes, I told you that you could have one piece out of my hand." So, he took the fifty cent piece - the largest gift in the man's hand, and, with a hearty "Thank you, sir," he was about to run off when the brother stopped him.

"I just want to ask you something, sonny. You took the biggest gift I had in my hand, and I had hoped you would. There were other gifts there, smaller ones, but you took the largest one. Now, God has a great many gifts too. Some you take every day, because you can't help it - the air you breathe, the food you eat, the mother who loves and takes care of you. All these are gifts from God. Those gifts you accept. Many of them you can't live without.

"But God has given a much greater gift than those," and so he began to tell this boy about God's wonderful love in the gift of His dear Son, to save sinners from their sins and for the glories of heaven.

And he asked him the question that I want to ask you in closing: "Have you ever accepted God's greatest gift, and said with the apostle Paul: 'Thanks be to God for His unspeakable gift?'"

# Godly Jealousy

*"Would to God ye could bear with me a little in my folly: and indeed bear with me. For I am jealous over you with godly jealousy: for I have espoused you to one husband, that I may present you as a chaste virgin to Christ. But I fear, lest by any means, as the serpent beguiled Eve through his subtilty, so your minds should be corrupted from the simplicity that is in Christ."*

(2 Cor. 11:1-3)

I have been charged a few times in my life with being jealous, but I was sure I did not deserve that compliment. To be jealous is indeed an honour one might well crave, for it puts one into the very highest class of society.

Paul tells us here that he was jealous after the example of his God, who seven times is spoken of in the Old Testament as a jealous God. Since God is pure and holy, then jealousy must be a virtue instead of a vice. What my accuser meant, of course, was that I was envious.

Envy is a crime; jealousy is one of the greatest virtues. If you have never been jealous, then you are just a spineless jellyfish. In the Old Testament the word means either envy or jealousy and is translated by both of these. You see, both spring from the same source - love.

The one, envy, is generated by love of self and, so, is evil; the other, jealousy, is created by love of others, and, so, is good. It is not the passion itself that is wrong, but the purpose it has in view. I envy others because I want what they have. I am jealous because they want what is rightfully mine. Envy has just two parties in view; jealousy presupposes a triangle - the eternal triangle.

For instance, a husband rightfully is jealous of his wife. He loves her, and her love should be supremely towards him. So, when a third party comes in to win his wife's affection, or to try to do so, he should be jealous.

Our God is a jealous God, too. Having redeemed us with the precious blood of Christ, we are now His and His alone, and He is jealous when we turn away from Him and love another, or other things, more than Him. That's why He tells us not to love the world, nor the things that are in the world.

When a wife loves another than her husband, she becomes an adulteress in God's sight, and so we are told in the Word: "Ye adulterers and adulteresses; know ye not that the friendship of the world is enmity with God?" (James 4:4). That is what Paul means in our text.

The Church, like a bride, has been betrothed to Christ. The devil drew Eve's heart away from trust in, and love for, God; and Paul says he does not want the Corinthians to be beguiled in that way in their precious relationship to Christ. He is jealous over them for Christ's sake, and wants them to be wholly true to the Lord Jesus.

Nothing is easier than to drift away from the enjoyment of the love of Christ and, thus, to become cold in heart towards Him. At Ephesus, where everything seemed to be so bright and prosperous, the sad note is sounded that they had left their first love (Rev. 2:4).

An Oriental story goes like this: A lady, walking along the road, was overtaken by a handsome gentleman. He suited his pace to hers and walked by her side in conversation. By and by he said: "You are beautiful and lovely. I've fallen in love with you. Will you marry me?" "But," said she, "this is so sudden. You have only known me for a few minutes. You don't know anything about me yet. Look behind you. That is my sister coming up the road. Why don't you go and talk to her? She is far more beautiful than me." So he left her and joined the other lady.

But shortly he caught up again with the first woman and said: "Why did you lie to me? Your sister is not beautiful; she is downright ugly." "True," was her reply, "but why did you lie to me? You said you loved me. If you loved me, why did you go after another woman?"

Even so, we may say we love the Lord, and yet at times our other loves intrude, and our hearts grow cold towards the true Lover of our souls. That's why God is jealous; that's why Paul was jealous over the Corinthians and us; that's why I should be jealous to see to it that the Lord Jesus has the first place in my heart and life.

Listen to Song of Solomon 8:6: "Love is as strong as death; jealousy is cruel as the grave (as sheol)." Love's strength is like death's power - it is irresistible; it comes into human experience and breaks down every barrier. (I am thinking of God's love in Christ.) And, while death takes, sheol holds, and so it is likened to jealousy, for as the unseen holds the spirit when death comes in, so jealousy holds the loved one for whom Christ died. Having loved His own, He loves them to the end, and is jealous of any outsider coming in to mar that precious bond of love.

In connection with our blessed Lord: how strong was His death! Through death, He destroyed death. It is love, love divine, that brought Him to the Cross; a love not merely as strong as death, but infinitely stronger than death. When He died, hades, as it were, would claim His soul, but it could not hold Him. He rose, praise His Name! Death could not keep His body; hades could not hold His soul. He came forth victoriously and now holds the keys of death and of hades.

And, having redeemed us by His precious blood, He claims us altogether for Himself. Our body is His, 1 Cor. 6:20; and our soul is His, 1 Peter 4:19. Death and sheol are strong, but Christ is stronger. Sheol could hold, but Christ can hold more securely and wants us, whom He holds, for Himself. As James 4:5 says: "the Spirit that dwelleth in us lusteth (desireth) to (the point of) envy (jealousy)." The Holy Spirit wants us altogether for Christ; and so does He!

Dear fellow believer, do you respond to His love? Are you jealous that nothing shall come between you and your Saviour? Do you love Christ now as you did when first you trusted Him? Do you remember the thrill of first love, and is it as real now?

Do you remember the thrill of first love as the old gentleman did? He was told on his 86th birthday, by his mathematically-inclined nephew, that, since his birth, his heart had beaten 3,299,087,600 times. "That's wonderful," said the octogenarian, "but you made one slight mistake in your calculations, sonny; it actually is only 3,299,087,599 times." "Impossible!" says the nephew. "These modern mathematical wizard machines never make mistakes." "That may be so, but still it's wrong. You see, the machine does not know that my heart skipped a beat when I first fell in love with my beloved Nancy."

Did your heart skip a beat when first you saw and loved Him who loved you and gave Himself for you? If so, has that thrill gone sour, maybe? If a bit of the love of the world has crept in, the Lord is jealous over you. How marvellous it is that the Lord is jealous over me - over insignificant, worthless me!

A person who is jealous wants the object of his affections all for himself or herself. He not only won my love by dying for me, but He wants my love still. I am His and He is mine! His love towards me never grows cold. May I never allow Satan to rob me of my responsive love to Him!

Oftentimes, a jealous husband will treat the one he loves the most, his wife, when she is untrue to him, even more rudely than he will her paramour. Even so will God chastise His own, those over whom He is jealous, as well as take vengeance on their deceivers. In Numbers 25:11 we read of His jealousy against His own; and in Isaiah 42:13, poured forth on the enemies of Israel.

We read seven times in the Old Testament that God is a jealous God; and six out of those seven times, they were told not to worship other gods. The Lord values our adoration of Him.

Oh, love that wilt not let me go,
I rest my weary soul on Thee;
I give Thee back the life I owe,
That, in Thine ocean depths, its flow
May richer, fuller be.

"Set me as a seal upon Thine heart; as a seal upon Thine arm." Let His love be real to me and, thus, in me. Let His power sustain me by His mighty arm. Let my heart be wholly His!

# Let Down; Caught Up

*"In Damascus the governor under Aretas the king kept the city of the Damascenes with a garrison, desirous to apprehend me: and through a window in a basket was I let down by the wall, and escaped his hands.*

*"It is not expedient for me doubtless to glory. I will come to visions and revelations of the Lord. I knew a man in Christ above fourteen years ago (whether in the body, I cannot tell; or whether out of the body, I cannot tell: God knoweth;) such an one caught up to the third heaven.*

*"And I knew such a man, (whether in the body, or out of the body, I cannot tell: God knoweth;) how that he was caught up into paradise, and heard unspeakable words, which it is not lawful for a man to utter."*

(2 Cor. 11:32; 12:1-4)

Note the sharp contrast between the close of chapter 11 and the opening of chapter 12: Let down - caught up. Life is made up of those two, isn't it? The world talks of life as being full of ups and downs, but notice that Paul speaks the other way around - not of ups and downs, but of downs and ups. Praise God, for us who believe in Christ, the last move is an "up". As Paul was caught up here individually, so the whole Church shall one day be caught up together to meet the Lord in the air, so to be forever with the Lord (1 Thess. 4:16-17).

Paul's "down" was but a very short distance, from the house on the top of the city wall to the road outside; but his "up" was millions and billions of miles, into the presence of God Himself, into paradise, the third heaven.

How thrilling it is to realize that our downs, as believers, are so puny compared with the stupendous heights of bliss to which, by faith, we already now ascend, and to which we shall be taken in glorified bodies at the coming of our Lord!

Paul's down is a preview of our own. He did not know, as he tells twice over, whether he had his body with him or not, but at the rapture, we will know, for we are told to look for the Saviour, who will change this body of humiliation and fashion it like unto His own body of glory (Phil. 3:20-21).

We may learn some valuable lessons now, for our spiritual blessing, from Paul's experience. First of all, he could not tell if he was in the body or not when he took his flight into space. His journey into those realms of bliss lifted him above and beyond the consciousness of material bonds.

It is so with us as, by faith, we mount up with wings as eagles. In communion with Christ and divine realities, we are divorced from occupation with, or realization of, the material. Such experience is true christian science, not the spurious foolishness that goes by that name. It is true that occupation with Christ delivers the child of God from undue involvement with the demands of the human body, and lifts him to the enjoyment of spiritual joys.

Many and many a time, while revelling in the things of God, I have completely forgotten I even had a body. Spiritual feasting had taken the mind above mere physical demands. The reason Christians are sometimes sick is because their minds are engaged with thinking about their troubles or petty cares. Set your mind on things above, not on the earth, and you will find you will enjoy better health as a result. I have gone to a meeting with a severe pain or something else, and in five minutes it was totally forgotten while singing His praises or hearing His wonderful Word ministered. Don't be occupied too much with your body. Leave it, and enjoy the unspeakable glories of heaven which are not possible for a man to utter.

We may well look at Paul's experience as achieving victory over the dominion of the body, for the body might well stand for the "flesh", which in Scripture represents sinful man. Paul forgot that, too, on his trip to the glory. Occupation with Christ and the glories of God's grace lifts the soul from the demands of the flesh and its lusts. It lifts us above this world and its sordid influence. As it says in 2 Corinthians 3:18: "But we all, with open face beholding as in a glass the glory of the Lord, are changed into the same image from glory to glory, even as by the Spirit of the Lord."

Another lesson we may well note from this incident is that, though Paul had this sensational experience of being caught up into the very presence of the Lord, it did not deliver him from the sinful nature still within him. Upon his return to earth, we read, in the verses following our text, that he was given a thorn in the flesh, the messenger of Satan to buffet him, lest he should be exalted above measure, see v.7. His visit to heaven had not robbed him of the danger of possible pride.

This tells us that nothing, as long as we are in the body, can set the believer free from this tendency to sin. The believer is waiting for the redemption of the body - he doesn't have it yet. Self must be kept under, that Christ may be seen.

The remedy for victory over self is in soaring above the earth in touch with God. As Isaiah 40:31 bids us, "mount up with wings as eagles". Let's take those trips into heavenly orbit often, so we'll have something more to talk about to folks besides the weather.

# Paul's Prayer for the Ephesians

*"In whom ye also trusted, after that ye heard the word of truth, the gospel of your salvation: in whom also after that ye believed, ye were sealed with that holy Spirit of promise, which is the earnest of our inheritance until the redemption of the purchased possession, unto the praise of His glory.*

*"Wherefore I also, after I heard of your faith in the Lord Jesus, and love unto all the saints, cease not to give thanks for you, making mention of you in my prayers; that the God of our Lord Jesus Christ, the Father of glory, may give unto you the spirit of wisdom and revelation in the knowledge of Him:*

*"The eyes of your understanding being enlightened; that ye may know what is the hope of His calling, and what the riches of the glory of His inheritance in the saints, and what is the exceeding greatness of His power to us-ward who believe, according to the working of His mighty power, which He wrought in Christ, when He raised Him from the dead..."*

(Eph. 1:13-20)

There is a prayer by the apostle Paul in the first chapter of this letter to the Ephesians, as partially quoted above, and another in the third chapter. This prayer has in view the understanding of the believer; that in the third chapter, his appreciation of the love of God in Christ. Power is the keynote here; there, it is love. He prays here to the God of our Lord Jesus Christ, with the emphasis on power. There, he prays to the Father, with the emphasis on love. Here, the grasp of the basic doctrines of the truth concerning the Church is the topic of his prayer; there, the enjoyment and practical experience of them.

This portion deals with two inheritances - ours, in verses 11-14; and His, in verse 18. We, His saints, are God's inheritance. May we say that the trait we see so clearly in

man's makeup comes from God? We are never really
satisfied with things; neither is our God. His delights were
with the sons of men (Prov. 8:31).

Here is a little girl, playing with her doll. That's alright for
the time being, but she won't always be satisfied with a doll.
God has implanted in that child the nature and desires that
will some day make her a mother. Now she plays with her
doll, but the affection is all from one side. The child does
the talking; she smiles at her make-believe baby; she rocks it
to sleep. But the doll just looks at her with those blank glass
eyes; there is no reciprocation whatever.

But, some day, this same little girl will grow up, get
married, become a mother, and will hold a real live baby in
her arms. Now, all the love does not come from the mother;
there is a response on the part of the little one. She smiles
back, clasps her tiny arms around her mother's neck, and
whispers, "I love you." And she grows up, to bring gladness
(or sorrow, alas) to the heart of the loving parent.

It is even so with God. He made men because He desired
their responsive love and affection. He made them in His
own image and likeness, or else they never could enter into
His thoughts or respond to His love. Sin came in to destroy
this fellowship, but divine grace has more than restored the
primeval bliss, and we are now His inheritance.

His riches are found in His saints, as our text says. May we
not sadden His heart but, rather, gladden it by loving Him
in return for all His great love to us!

We *are* an inheritance - God's inheritance; and we *have*
an inheritance - our inheritance. We have the earnest of the
Spirit because we have an inheritance; we are sealed with
the Spirit because we are His inheritance. The sealing
secures us for God; the earnest enables us to enjoy already
now, by faith, the riches of our spiritual inheritance.

Some day we shall be taken to heaven, which event is
called, in verse 14, the redemption of the purchased
possession, when Christ, at the rapture, shall redeem our
bodies, which He purchased with His precious blood at
Calvary. Till that day comes, God has given us His Holy Spirit
as an earnest, a down payment, as it were, or a foretaste of

the eternal riches that are ours in Christ.

Right now, we haven't got sense enough to handle our vast wealth, so the Spirit gives us what He knows we are able to enjoy and to use well. It is something like this: A rich heiress I knew once was under age, and was under the control of guardians, who in turn operated under the supervision of the court. Upon coming of age, she would inherit millions, but in the meantime, her fortune was doled out to her in small yearly installments. I remember her guardians being in court, seeking a larger allowance for the girl, saying she could not possibly live on the meagre $40.00 a year she was then getting.

Now, I understand that, in cases like that, the judge considers every circumstance. If the minor uses her money well and wisely, the court may agree to increase the yearly amount; if she wastes it in foolish living, he may cut it down.

I believe that our God does something similar in our case. If we enjoy the riches of God's Word and use them well, the Spirit will give us more, for the Bible says that to him that hath shall more be given. But, if we do not feed on the precious things of God's Word and value them; or if we do not spend them freely in sharing them with others, we will get less. The Spirit loves to have us appreciate Christ and His grace.

Then, there is the seal of the Spirit. We seal things for security because they are valuable. Only the party to whom the letter or parcel is addressed has the right to break that seal. That means that the believer cannot possibly be lost, for only God can break the seal. As Ephesians 4:30 puts it, we are sealed by the Holy Spirit of God until the day of redemption.

As we said, we seal things because they are valuable. Isn't it a precious thought, then, that we are so valuable to God that He personally seals us with His Spirit, for we are sealed not by, but with His Spirit - the Spirit Himself is the seal. Who am I? I'm certainly not worth anything. That's true enough.

I heard a preacher say one time that he was staying as a guest in a wealthy home. He noticed, among all the lovely furnishings and bric-a-brac, a rather ugly, cheap-looking piece of pottery standing on the mantle shelf in the living room. It looked so out of place amidst those gorgeous surroundings that he felt tempted to hide it behind a picture somewhere so it would not be seen.

But, one day the lady of the house saw him looking at it, and said to him, "That's a very valuable piece. It is from a very rare dynasty in China, where my husband bought it when we lived there." She told him it cost many thousands of dollars. After that, though it still looked just as ugly to him, the gentleman regarded it with some awe and respect. He didn't even go near it again, for fear even his breath might knock it off the ledge. It was the same homely piece, but see what it cost. It was valued, not by its intrinsic value, but by the price it would bring.

This is how God looks at us. He values us at the price paid for us, though, in ourselves, we are nothing. We have been bought with the highest price ever paid in the universe. Our blessed Lord gave Himself for us, a price that surpasses all temporal or eternal estimates. That's why we are sealed. God just can't afford to lose us, after such a tremendous cost.

And, praise His Name, we are not always going to remain ugly. The rich owner could not do much about the appearance of the ugly vase, but God can and will do a great deal about our looks. Ephesians 5:27 tells us that He will remove every spot and wrinkle, and shall present us all glorious to Himself in that day of glory that awaits the believer in Jesus. All glory to His Name!

# Paul's other Prayer for the Ephesians

*"For this cause I bow my knees unto the Father of our Lord Jesus Christ, of whom the whole family in heaven and earth is named, that He would grant you, according to the riches of His glory, to be strengthened with might by His Spirit in the inner man;*

*"That Christ may dwell in your hearts by faith; that ye, being rooted and grounded in love, may be able to comprehend with all saints what is the breadth, and length, and depth, and height;*

*"And to know the love of Christ, which passeth knowledge, that ye might be filled with all the fulness of God. Now unto Him that is able to do exceeding abundantly above all that we ask or think, according to the power that worketh in us, unto Him be glory in the Church by Christ Jesus throughout all ages, world without end. Amen."*

(Eph. 3: 14-21)

At the conclusion of Paul's masterful setting forth of the great doctrines of the Church, he prays that the saints might be able to enter into the appreciation of them; that they may know and grow; dwell and comprehend. That the whole man, the inner man, with special emphasis on the heart and mind, might be filled into (not with) all the fulness of God.

Here truly is a challenge to the earnest seeker after hidden treasures. Here the Spirit seeks to arouse a noble ambition in the believer's heart and mind to soar up into the limitless heights of divine revelation, so that Christ may be known to the Church and through the Church, now and forevermore.

Paul prays first that the believer may be strengthened with might by the Spirit in the inner man. This does not refer to the body, though folks talk about going to feed the inner man when they sit down to a meal. That is the outer man.

2 Corinthians 4:16 tells us that the outward man perishes (that is, the body grows weaker and eventually dies), but the inward man is renewed day by day. The inner man is the believer, born again by the grace of God, the new man, his real spiritual self. Physically, a believer grows older, but spiritually he grows younger; he is renewed day by day.

In Florida, where I live, among other points of interest they will show you (if you are interested in sightseeing) is Ponce de Leon's fountain of eternal youth in St. Augustine. The legend is that the explorer discovered this well and that one drink of it would ensure eternal vigour and youthfulness. I doubt whether it worked, for no one has seen that explorer lately, and he is supposed to have drunk from that fountain.

No, there is no such thing as a fountain of eternal youth down here on earth as such, but, praise God, there is such a fountain for the believer in Jesus. Take but one drink of the water of life and God assures you that you shall live forever.

As our Saviour told that Samaritan woman: "Whosoever drinketh of this water shall thirst again: But whosoever drinketh of the water that I shall give him shall never thirst; but the water that I shall give him shall be in him a well of water springing up into everlasting life" (John 4:13-14). That fountain of eternal youth not only quenches the thirst of the drinker and gives him eternal life, but also is instrumental in meeting the need of others, as well. Praise God, the believer has the dew of eternal youth!

Then Paul prays that Christ may dwell in our hearts by faith. He prays here first for the heart, verse 17; and then, in verse 18, he prays for the mind. The heart comes first, in God's reckoning.

When I was a young man, they used to say, in the plant where I worked, that a man was worth $3.00 a day from his shoulders down. What he had from his shoulders higher would determine his real worth. His brain, not his brawn, counted most.

But, with God, the reverse is true. With Him, the heart is most important - that which is below the shoulders, not above. No matter what a Christian does, if it is not the outflow of love and devotion to Christ, it is of no value in the sight of God. The first three verses of 1 Corinthians 13 tell us this in no uncertain terms. Our service may be very earnest, may be correct enough and even fruitful, yet if it lacks what our Lord values most, love to Christ, it is like sounding brass or a tinkling cymbal.

There is a precious example of true, acceptable homage in Luke 7. You remember that the Lord had been invited over by Simon the Pharisee, and that a sinful woman had come in and washed the Lord's feet with tears and then wiped them with the hairs of her head. When the Pharisee inwardly began to criticize the Saviour for permitting a known sinner to touch Him, Jesus (reading his thoughts) said: "Simon, I have somewhat to say unto thee. Seest thou this woman? I entered into thine house, thou gavest Me no water for My feet (which was an act of discourtesy almost unbelievable in that day): but she hath washed My feet with tears, and wiped them with the hairs of her head."

Now, suppose Simon had seen to it that the Lord's feet had been washed; no doubt he would have gotten the water out of the well. It would have been cold water from the outside, but the woman washed Jesus' feet with hot water from the inside, with her tears. Our activities in the service of our Lord often may be correct enough, but cold and formal; with this woman, it was the expression of a soul deeply moved by Christ's love to her. She loved much, because she appreciated His love so much.

Now Paul prays that the saints may be able to comprehend the breadth and length and depth and height. He prays that the mind, enlightened by the Spirit, may be able to grasp the fathomless mysteries of the christian faith, enjoy them, be affected by them in their daily lives, and be able to make them precious and real to others, as they minister God's Word to such.

Here we see breadth without any side; length without end; depth without any bottom; height without any top.

Here the believer may soar, by faith, into the vast wonders unfolded by the Spirit and enfolded in God's holy Word. Here we are called upon to know the bliss of fourth-dimensional living.

As the second dimension carries us from a mere line into surface (for length and breadth form surface); and as the third dimension takes us from mere flat surface into substance (for all physical, material matter is three-dimensional), so the fourth dimension would carry us beyond the physical into the ethereal - into the spiritual.

Our Lord, after He rose from the dead, had, as it were, a fourth-dimensional body, for it was not limited by time, space or matter. He could go through solid doors, ascend to heaven (those billions upon billions of miles) in a moment, appear and disappear at will, etc. Some day we, too, shall have such capacities, but, praise God, right now we do have the ability to live a fourth-dimensional spiritual life. While our bodies are confined to this earth, our souls and spirits soar into realms of heavenly glory and delight. As Isaiah 40:31 says, we "mount up with wings as eagles".

A brother and I were driving through the country near Milwaukee, Wisconsin years ago when we passed a farm. As we did so, a horse stuck its head over the high stone wall surrounding the barn yard. I said to the friend with me: "Why do you think that horse is looking over the wall?" "I don't know exactly," said he. I asked, "Don't you think it is because he can't look through it?" "Oh, of course," said he, "everybody knows that." "Yes, true, but you didn't seem to think of that," said I.

√    That horse teaches us a good lesson. Don't try to look through troubles; look over them. Use a little horse sense. So often we live our lives on a horizontal level, instead of soaring above the clouds to tell our cares to our Lord or to enjoy communion with Him. Here below, we are still in the body pent, but our souls and spirits are as free as the birds of the air. It has been said that neither beds, nor bars, nor bonds, nor bodies need to keep us from enjoying the infinite resources of God's marvellous grace.

Then the prayer goes on to wish that the believer might

know the love of Christ, which passeth knowing. A contradiction? No, indeed. We know, and yet we never know. The love of Christ is ever beyond us.

Sometimes I have introduced my wife to folks at some special gathering of believers, and perhaps someone would say: "Oh, I know your wife; I met her two years ago at such and such a place." And I tell them: "You're doing wonderfully! You met my wife once and you know her! I've lived with her for over fifty years, and I don't know her yet, and don't think I ever will know her fully."

That's what makes the knowledge of Christ so wonderful. There is ever more to learn. Through the eternal ages, He will show the exceeding riches of His grace in His kindness toward us through Christ Jesus (Eph. 2:7).

A little boy, who lived away inland, had the privilege of spending a vacation at the seashore. Coming back to school, he boasted to his chums that he had seen the ocean. He was right and wrong at the same time. True, he had seen the sea, but how much of it? Just as much as his vision could reach, but there were thousands of miles beyond it. He had seen it, perhaps, placidly calm, but not in its fury, breaking on the rocks.

So it is with the love of Christ. The ocean of God's love ever beckons us to further exploration. Unlike the sea somewhere down here, it never presents the same view; there is endless variation to intrigue and delight the searcher after heaven's glories.

"To know the love of Christ...that ye might be filled with all the fulness of God." It should read to be filled "into" all the fulness of God. It is quite evident that we could not possibly be filled with God's fulness - our little cup cannot contain His eternal vastness. The ocean can never be exhausted, no matter how much I may draw upon it.

I heard of an elderly man who had been advised by his doctor to go to the seashore and, for some affliction which he had, to soak his feet each morning in salt water from the ocean, after warming it. So, every morning he went down to the beach nearby and dipped a pail of water and carried it to his cottage.

It so happened that another man, a drifter, saw him do this morning after morning, and about the seventh or eighth morning, he just could not take this any more. So, looking at the old gentleman, he said, as he shook his head: "You'll never do it; you'll never do it." He thought the other man was trying to empty the ocean a pail at a time. You might as well expect to exhaust God's infinite fulness with your little cup. Keep on dipping - there's always more!

*But though I cannot tell or sing or know*
*The fulness of Thy love while here below,*
*My empty vessel I may freely bring-*
*O Thou, who art of love the living spring,*
*My vessel fill.*

I heard a tale of a London cockney who had the chance to spend a week at the seashore, through the kindness of a mission he attended. His wife was ill and not able to go along. So, toward the end of his stay, he wondered whether he could take her a memento of his visit. He finally decided he would take a bottle of ocean water with him, so she could at least see, smell and taste that which he had so delighted bathing in.

He mentioned his plan to a man sitting by him on the beach, who decided he might as well take advantage of the ignorance of the other. "Yes, that's fine," said he, "but you can't just take the water, you know; it costs money. I am in charge of selling it; I'll sell you a bottle full of it for a shilling." So, the man paid for the water and took it home.

Early the next morning, he was back at the beach for a last look before returning to the city. He had bought the water the evening before, when the tide was high; now it was low. Looking at the long width of dry beach and the low water, he said to the cheat of the night before: "Say, you must have done a lot of business since last night, eh?" But, if he had come back that evening, he would have seen the water as high as it was the night before.

Sometimes believers fail to rejoice in the Lord - the tide is low, as it were; but the next day it will be high again. Let's dip our tiny cup into the ocean of His love. Yes, not only to have it filled, but that it may overflow in praise to God and service to man, Psalm 23:5.

In this wonderful portion of God's Word, we have:

Endowment - the riches of His grace - verse 16.

Enduement - strengthened by His Spirit - verse 16.

Enthronement - Christ dwelling in the heart - verse 17.

Establishment - rooted and grounded in love - verse 17.

Enlightenment - to comprehend - verse 18.

Enjoyment - to know the love of Christ - verse 19.

Enrichment - filled into all the fulness of God -verse 19.

# Spiritual Gifts (i)

*"But unto every one of us is given grace according to the measure of the gift of Christ."*

(Eph. 4:7)

*"As every man hath received the gift, even so minister the same one to another, as good stewards of the manifold grace of God."*

(1 Peter 4:10)

*"Now there are diversities of gifts, but the same Spirit...But all these worketh that one and the selfsame Spirit, dividing to every man severally as He will."*

(1 Cor. 12:4, 11)

Every believer has been given one or more gifts to be used for the glory of God. These gifts are to be used to help and encourage fellow believers, as well as in the ministry of the gospel. 1 Corinthians 12:18 says that God has set the members, every one of them, in the Body as it has pleased Him. Just as in the human body every member performs a different function, such as the eye, the hand, the mouth, etc., so in the Body, the Church.

No two members are exactly alike, and each one is useful and needed in his or her particular place. Some members in the human body are more prominent than others; some perform more important functions; but all alike fill a place that is vital to the welfare of the whole. It is so in the Church.

It might be well to note that, in the human body, the most important organs, such as the heart, the liver, the stomach, etc., are out of sight. One could get along without a face, or without hands or feet, but it is impossible to manage without a heart. So, in spiritual life it is not always, by any means, the believers who are in the limelight who perform the most needed service. As 1 Corinthians 12:24-25 says: "For our comely parts have no need: but God hath tempered the body together, having given more abundant honour to that part which lacked: That there should be no schism in the body; but that the members should have the same care one for another."

That statement simply means that God often magnifies the importance of a lowly ministry and minimizes the importance of the prominent, that thus believers might work together in harmony and unity. These verses prevent a superiority complex on the one hand, and an inferiority complex on the other, so that the humble may be encouraged, and the proud humbled. Just remember there is only one "you" in the whole wide world. For each believer in Jesus, He has a special place for them to fill.

At a conference of believers, a very gifted speaker delivered a forceful and stirring address. When he sat down, another brother arose and said: "After listening to this splendid message, I would not get up at all if it weren't for the fact that I always remind myself that nobody on earth can preach like I can." To safeguard against any misapprehension, he added: "My preaching is poor enough; nevertheless, there is no one on earth who can preach just as I do it." Of course, he was right. Just be yourself. Use the gift God has given you, whether in preaching, in personal work, in singing, or whatever else. As one black brother said: "Jus' be what yo' is and not what yo' ain't, for if yo' is what yo' ain't, then yo ain't what yo' is!"

Always remember that we are to minister our gift as good stewards of the manifold grace of God.

I read once that a lady was giving an organ recital in a church in the days when electricity was as yet unknown, when the organ bellows had to be pumped by elbow grease. After she had played a lovely piece, the audience vociferously applauded.

When the applause had died down, the young fellow who had pumped the bellows said to her: "My, we played that piece beautifully, didn't we?" "We?" she said scornfully. "You mean I did." The boy did not say any more, but when the time came for the next selection and the organist put her hands on the keys, there wasn't a sound.

"Go on and pump the bellows," whispered she to the lackey. "I will," said he, "after we settle the little argument we had just now. Who played that last piece - you or we?" "Alright," she grinned, "we did, I guess." "Fine," said he, "then I'll pump again." Of course, the skill of the artist was much greater than that of the boy who did the menial work, but it was not any more vital.

Your ministry is as much needed as mine. In the day when the Judgment Seat of Christ is set, God is not going to reward the believer for success, or skill, or ability, or results, but for faithfulness. The humblest housewife will receive as great a reward as the mightiest preacher who ever lived, if she has been as faithful in her sphere as he has been in his. Perhaps she will receive greater praise, for the preacher receives a good deal of praise here and now. Perhaps, as the Lord said of the Pharisees in Matthew 6 (who relished the praise of men): "they have their reward".

If you want to serve the Lord in a wider sphere, then brighten the corner where you are. Jesus said: "to him that hath shall more be given"; and in 1 Corinthians 12:31: "Covet earnestly the best gifts."

# Three Unities

*"Endeavoring to keep the unity of the Spirit in the bond of peace. There is one body, and one Spirit...Till we all come in the unity of the faith, and of the knowledge of the Son of God, unto a perfect man..."*

(Eph. 4:3, 4, 13)

There are three unities in these three verses. The body is a unity, there is the unity of the Spirit and the unity of the faith.

The Church of God is likened so often by Paul to a human body. It is a divine organism, even as the human body is. Though composed of many members, yet it is an entity, one organic whole. The true Church of Scripture, composed of believers in Jesus only, is not an organization, but an organism. An organization is a conglomeration of separate parts or parties, with no vital link with each other; it is a thing without any life. But an organism is formed of many parts indissolubly and inextricably connected with each other, controlled by the head and activated by one common pervading force - life. The human body is such; so is the Church.

The Church is a unity, not a union. It has been said that you could tie the tails of two cats together and then hang them over a clothesline. You'd have union, but I guarantee you would not have unity. A man and his wife are one when united in marriage. They have formed a union, but that's not unity. Their characters might be completely divergent, and they might fight like cats and dogs. They are united, but do not have the same life and nature.

Then, again, the Church is a unity, not a uniformity. You have uniformity in a jail, or in the army, but that isn't unity, either. There they all do alike, often even dress alike. Sometimes Christians seem to think that unity implies that all believers are to look at things alike and act alike; but unity implies the exact opposite.

A body is a unity, and in a human body no two members act the same way. Unity is actually diversity. A unity is that in which each part does something else, but where all is done for the good of the whole, and where life actuates the whole.

The Church of God is composed of many individual members, yet all united together by the same Spirit of life into one organic whole, where each member performs his or her appointed task for the spiritual welfare and usefulness in the service of Christ.

Through the Body, the Church, Christ is made known to the world around. So that this Body might grow strong and be capable of doing its duties, God has given gifts to it - evangelists, pastors and teachers; and gifts in it, as we saw in our previous article.

# Spiritual Gifts (ii)

*"And He gave some, apostles; and some, prophets; and some, evangelists; and some, pastors and teachers; for the perfecting of the saints, for the work of the ministry, for the edifying of the body of Christ:*

*"Till we all come in the unity of the faith, and of the knowledge of the Son of God, unto a perfect man, unto the measure of the stature of the fulness of Christ: that we henceforth be no more children, tossed to and fro, and carried about with every wind of doctrine, by the sleight of men, and cunning craftiness, whereby they lie in wait to deceive;*

*"But speaking the truth in love, may grow up into Him in all things, which is the Head, even Christ: from whom*

*the whole Body fitly joined together and compacted by that*
*which every joint supplieth, according to the effectual*
*working in the measure of every part, maketh increase of*
*the Body unto the edifying of itself in love."*

(Eph. 4:11-16)

God gave gifted men to the Church, and He still does, to
minister the Word to the saints, so that they themselves may
be built up and fitted for the work of the ministry in their
turn. Teachers are given so that believers may become able
to teach, as we read in Hebrews 5:12, "For when for the
time ye ought to be teachers." Having profited by the
ministry of the Word, every Christian should be able to
contribute something so that the whole Church may grow
spiritually, in grace and in the knowledge of Christ. That
idea is developed in that magnificent verse 16 of our
present text.

Just as in the human body every member works to keep
the whole in health and vigour, so should it be in the
assembly of the saints. The first thing we might notice is that
every member contributes - every joint supplies. There are
folks who only come to meetings for what they can get, and
who grumble when the fare is meagre. Christianity is not
based on getting, but on giving.

Years ago a brother said to me: "Oh, I don't come to the
weeknight meetings. I don't get anything there. When I go
to hear some prominent speaker, I get a square meal; but in
our assembly gatherings, I don't even get a light lunch."
Said I to him: "What do you do with those good dinners you
get? You say you get square meals, and I only get light
lunches; yet I teach a Sunday School class, I preach in the
open air several times a week, I preach in country
schoolhouses, and I visit the sick; but you do nothing, as far
as I know. Those square meals seem to leave you awfully
weak.

"You remind me of a horse I once owned. I bought a
small 20-acre farm in my foolish days, and a sharp farmer
sold me a horse for $80.00. The horse's name was "May",
but after I had her for a week or two, I named her "Maybe",

for you never could tell whether she would go or not. That horse was always eating, yet it was so weak it could hardly stand up. It had a distemper of some sort.

"One night I drove into town to go to meet with the Lord's people, and that horse fell down in the shafts of the buggy. The cop talked about arresting me for cruelty to animals in not feeding the beast as I should have. 'Feeding it?' said I to him. 'That horse is eating from morning till night. I fed it almost a full pail of oats this morning. When I drove just a short distance to see a farmer about something, I tied the horse at the barn door. When I came back, it had eaten all the straw off the barn floor and an old broom that stood there, and was just starting on the handle. That horse is always eating! When I got home, I fed it some more oats, and yet tonight it fell down from pure weakness.'

"You," said I to that critical brother, "are like that horse of mine. You are always eating, always feasting on good things, yet you are so weak you are unable to do anything for the Lord. You've got the wrong psychology. You're not supposed to come to meetings to get, but to give! You'll never grow in grace and in the knowledge of Christ unless you learn to contribute."

A little boy was watching an electric linesman work on a power line. Said the inquisitive squirt: "Say, mister, what are you doing wearing rubber boots? It ain't raining." "I am not wearing these boots because it is raining," said the man, "but because I am touching this high voltage wire up here. You see, sonny, I can touch this deadly wire with my bare hands, but if I did not wear these rubbers, I would get killed just like that! These rubber boots keep the electric power from going out of me, and once it can't get out, it can't get into me, either."

So it is with the precious truths of God's Word. They won't get into you unless they get out again. There has to be a circuit. Pass on the things you enjoy from the Word; that's the way they will really become yours, and you'll grow by them.

We sing that hymn, "Nothing in my hand I bring", and that's nice. But that's true only of sinners when they come to Christ to be saved; it is never to be true of saints when they come to Him. Priests were consecrated to the Lord in the Old Testament, and that word "consecrated" literally means to "have the hands filled".

We should take heed to the words from the Lord that Moses told the children of Israel: "None shall appear before Me empty" (Exod. 23:15).

Coming out from the morning service, one pious brother said unctuously: "We have a wonderful pastor. I have nothing but praise for our preacher." "That's what I noticed," dryly said the deacon who had passed him the collection plate.

In that wonderful verse 16 of our text, the graphic illustration is used of how each member of our human body is a contributing factor to the welfare of the whole body, and that this is so when saints meet together, as the Body of Christ, for mutual edification, according to God's order.

When I am asked over to a home, perhaps after an evening meeting, the lady of the house soon asks me: "Brother, would you like a dish of ice cream?" Now, it so happens that I like ice cream, and so, immediately, at least three members of my body get busy. My ears hear her question; my lips respond with a "Yes, thank you," and, in anticipation of the forthcoming treat, my stomach already starts to churn (as those who ought to know tell me).

So, the lady brings in the ice cream, and another member of my body gets into the act - my eyes. I see the ice cream; but then, you can't take in ice cream through your eyes, so my eyes send a wireless back to headquarters and say: "There's ice cream coming! What am I going to do about it?" And my brain sends back the message to my hand and says, "Put out your hand and take the ice cream." But again, you can't eat ice cream with your hand, so once more there is a swift communication with headquarters, the control board, and the hand gets the order: "Pass that ice cream on to your lips, stupid."

But that does not help much, either, for it would only melt there and make a mess, so again the wires get busy and the next order comes for the lips to pass the ice cream on further to the mouth, the palate, the throat, the oesophagus, the stomach, and goodness only knows where it goes after that; I surely don't. However, eventually that ice cream gets into the bloodstream and every part of my body, to the very roots of my hair - even the extreme limit of my little toes gets an infinitesimal fraction of the benefit of that ice cream.

But, and here lies the force of this parable, no member of my body could have had any of that ice cream if it had kept the ice cream in its grasp. The secret of success lay in the fact that "every member passed it on".

The only way to get, therefore, is to give. No member is sufficient to itself; all are interdependent on each other. Christians meet, share together what they have learned and valued from God's Word, which is the food of our souls, and thus they grow.

Please note that, in this very operation, two vital functions in regard to growth are present - one is food, the other is exercise. Each member does something; each member gets something. Just as, physically, a person develops through food and exercise, so it is in the spiritual. Some Christians overemphasize the exercise; others, the feeding; both should be kept in proper balance.

A new minister came to a congregation, and one of the greasiest members said to the new pastor: "I hope you have come to feed the flock." Looking at him, the preacher replied: "Brother, by the looks of you, what you need is not food, but exercise!"

Don't sit on the sidelines and criticize; any fool can do that. Contribute something. Remember that little is much when God is in it.

In a certain town, there lived a man named Little. He lived in a little town, on a little street, in a little house, and on a little salary. And besides him and Mrs. Little, there were seven little Littles. One day a friend said to him: "Mr. Little, how do you and Mrs. Little and all those little Littles manage to get by on such a little salary?" And, of course, you know what he said: "Every Little helps."

Don't forget it! Just be content to be a little Little until you grow bigger. A certain brother, in pseudo-modesty and humility, used to pray: "Oh, Lord, make me content just to be a doormat for my brethren." Then, one day a brother stepped on him pretty hard and did he blow up! Another brother, hearing him, said: "This is the first time in my life I ever heard a doormat squeal!"

# Fullness of the Spirit

*"And be not drunk with wine, wherein is excess; but be filled with the Spirit."*

(Eph. 5:18)

We are never told to be baptized with the Spirit, or to be born again of the Spirit, or to be sealed with the Spirit, for those, and other ministries of the Holy Spirit, are true of all believers. But we are exhorted, as in our text, to seek the fulness or power of the Spirit.

The verb "filled" is in the present continuous mood, suggesting that we should constantly be full of the Spirit. Our life should not be a spasmodic one, up in the clouds today and down in the dumps tomorrow. We should be controlled by the Spirit all the time. As has been said, we have the Spirit, but does He have us? We have the Holy Spirit indwelling us; He is resident in us, but is He the President of our lives? How are we to be filled with the Spirit?

I heard a preacher once use this illustration in this regard: he had a glass standing on the desk, and also a jug of water. Lifting the glass, he asked his hearers, "Is there anything in this glass?" Some said there wasn't, but he said, "Oh yes, there is; there is no such thing as a vacuum. This glass is not empty; it is full of air. Now," said he, "how shall I get this air out? Very simply, indeed." He took the jug of water and slowly filled the glass to the brim. "Now," said he, "the water has driven the air out; even so, the coming in of the Holy Spirit will drive out what is not of God."

As I listened to this, I could not help saying to myself that his illustration did not really illustrate anything; it was not true to life. It might have been alright if our hearts were filled with air (some folks are full of hot air, I know), but they are not. Suppose, said I to myself, that glass had been half full of dirt or junk of some kind. Then, pouring in the water would not have driven that out.

The hearts of believers are often filled with many things not pleasing to our Lord. It is first necessary to empty out the junk before the Spirit can come in. Read the opening verses of Ephesians 5, and you'll see how we are urged to clean up first, for it is clean vessels the Lord wants to use. The Spirit would not fill a believer who harbours sin in any form in his life, whether it be moral or spiritual evil. These will have to be cast out first. This is the secret to the obtaining of the fulness of the Spirit. It follows confession and self-judgment and turning from sin.

Another illustration will confirm this. I plant a number of tomato plants in my garden. In a week or two, those young plants are almost lost in a perfect maze of weeds. What do I do? I don't go into that plot of ground and pat those cute little weeds on the head and tell them how delighted I am to have them as my guests. No, indeed, I go into that field with murder in my soul.

I pluck up those wretched trespassers and stamp on them. I have to do it if I am going to raise any tomatoes. Weeds need no encouragement. If I never plant or cultivate another weed, the pests will grow anyway, but worthwhile plants or flowers need to be tended all the time. After a week or two, I find a lot more weeds in my vegetable garden, and I tear them up some more. Then, after a while, the tomato plants grow so big and strong that the weeds are crowded out by them, to a large extent. This is an exact parable of the christian life.

The weeds typify sins, the bad habits, the selfwill, which

are all the products of the old sinful nature. If I want to produce fruit in my life for the glory of God, I must unmercifully tear up those sinful things. In other words, I must exercise unsparing self-judgment, confessing my sins and failures before God. In that way, room is made for the Spirit to take His rightful place in my heart and life, thus to produce good fruit, as I did with my tomatoes.

The trouble is that, so often, believers, instead of judging sin in themselves, excuse it. They can be very hard on others, yet very easy on themselves. The exact reverse should be true. We should unmercifully judge ourselves, but exercise pity and endless patience with the faults of others. We must not have pity on the weeds, or they will stay with us.

One day a lady said to Billy Sunday: "I've got a bad temper, but there's one thing about me: I'm quick up, but quick down, too. I don't stay mad." You see, she was really excusing herself, instead of honestly condemning herself. Billy Sunday replied: "Yes, ma'am, you're quick up and down; so is a shotgun, but it does a lot of damage while it's blowing off!"

I knew a young preacher many years ago who fell into a grievous sin. Knowing him well, I went to see him and talked to him about this, and he readily admitted his guilt. "But," said he, "you know the Scripture says that the spirit is willing, but the flesh is weak." You see, he, too, was excusing himself in making that quotation.

"Oh, no," I said to him, "you did not commit that sin because the flesh is weak, but because it is strong. You are taking Scripture out of its context and misapplying it, trying to excuse yourself. The words you just quoted were not spoken by a sinner, but by the Saviour. They were not used by Simon Peter as an excuse after he had denied the Lord, but by the Lord Jesus as a warning before he did. They were not meant as an excuse, but as a warning."

The Lord was not talking about the flesh as a sinful entity, but of flesh as illustrating that man, by nature, is weak - not sinful in this connection. He was reminding Peter that, as a weak human being, he needed Divine strength to be able to stand. He was advised by the Lord to pray. He didn't; so, when the test came, he failed. Jesus did pray in Gethsemane, and when His trial came, He was triumphantly victorious.

We might note, in closing, that this fulness of the Spirit does not necessarily predicate the performance of some notable exploits. It does not have in view some amazing miracles, or some mighty power in preaching. No, it is for the purpose that the believer might be full of joy, making melody in his heart to the Lord, and giving thanks always, while submitting himself/herself to fellow saints, instead of seeking a place for one's self.

# Church as Bride

*"Husbands, love your wives, even as Christ also loved the Church, and gave Himself for it; that He might sanctify and cleanse it with the washing of water by the Word, that He might present it to Himself a glorious Church, not having spot, or wrinkle, or any such thing; but that it should be holy and without blemish."*

(Eph. 5:25-27)

Three chief figures are used for the Church in this exalted epistle to the Ephesians - that of a Body, a Building and a Bride. These three, as it were, bid us to look at the Church in the past, the present and the future.

As a Body (typified by a human body), the Church, as it were, was born at Pentecost, even as a human body has its start at birth. A body is complete at birth, with all the members there. It grows in size during the years, and in mental and spiritual capacity, but not in its parts, which are all there the day the baby is born. So, the Church, as a Body, is pictured as ever being complete in the eyes of God.

As a building, it is being added to day by day, even as a building is never complete till the last stone is added, and the last work is done. It pictures the Church in its present state of growing numerically, as souls are saved, and as living stones are placed in that great spiritual structure, as we read in Ephesians 2:21: "...all the building fitly framed together groweth unto an holy temple in the Lord".

With the Church as a Bride, the eye of faith is bidden to look onward, for the Church will not be His Bride in actual consummation until the wedding day; and that nuptial day shall not come till the Lord has come and caught His redeemed people home to the Glory. Then, up there with Him, the blessed nuptial day shall dawn. As we read in Revelation 19:7: "Let us be glad and rejoice, and give honour to Him: for the marriage of the Lamb is come, and His wife hath made herself ready".

It is through our body that we live our life, so that the Church as a Body intimates a life of service and devotion. As Christ, in His body down here, made God known, so does the Church, as His Body, make Christ known. Thus, in the body simile, we have the thought of "service".

In a building, the thought is that of "communion", for He dwells there in the midst of His own, whether that building be a home where the family meets together, or a temple where the believers worship Him.

As a Bride, the thought, of course, is that of the closest possible intimacy of love, personal enjoyment and delight.

In our text the emphasis is on the blessed ministry of Christ in relation to His Bride, the Church. Verse 32 assures us that the things the apostle writes, in regard to this subject, are a "great mystery"; but he speaks concerning Christ and the Church, thus likening the Church to a wife and Christ to her Husband - see verse 25.

In the three verses of our text, the Spirit calls our attention to our blessed Lord in His love for His own in the past, the present and the future. As to the past, He gave Himself for her; as to the present, He nourishes and

cherishes her; as to the future, He will present her to
Himself, a glorious Bride.

1. He loved the Church before she existed; He died for
her before she was ever brought into being. That
tremendous act had been conceived in the counsels of
eternity and, in the garden of Eden, had been foreshadowed
in the formation of Eve from Adam's side, and in her union
with him, as verses 31-32 of our chapter declare so plainly.
He bought His Bride at the infinite cost of His life laid down,
paying for her sins, shedding His precious blood (Acts
20:28). As Boaz could say: "I have purchased Ruth to be my
wife", so our far greater Boaz bought His wife with a far
greater price.

2. Now He is, in constant unwavering love, separating His
loved Church from defilement with the world, cleansing her
with the Word (as the Spirit applies that Word to the believer
each day), and nourishing and cherishing her. As a lover
whispers words of endearment to his beloved, so Christ
cherishes (or courts, we might say) His Bride. Through His
Word, He ever assures us of His deep affection, so as to keep
us close to Himself and true to Him.

3. Bye and bye, when He comes to take us Home, He will
present us to Himself. At that wonderful wedding, all the
attention will be focused on the Bridegroom. He will be
both the Bridegroom and the Best Man, for He presents the
Bride to Himself; even the Father is not mentioned at the
wedding. The Bride will be beautiful indeed, without spot
or wrinkle, but it is the Bridegroom who will fill the scene.

*The Bride eyes not her garment,*
*But her dear Bridegroom's face;*
*She will not gaze at glory,*
*But on her King of Grace.*

Yet, the Bride, too, will be very lovely. All the stains of sin
will be completely erased. How marvellous is the grace and
power of God!

When I got married, I sent my father in the old country
the picture taken of my bride and me together. When he

wrote back, he said, among other things: "You are always complaining about your eyesight, but, to judge by this photograph, there is nothing wrong with your sight." And, to tell you the truth, I agreed with him 100%. She was indeed lovely to look at, with her beautifully smooth skin, her dark expressive eyes, her glorious hair. Oh, well, why say more? You know what I mean.

But many years have since passed, and great changes have taken place, since that day, in the physical appearance of my bride. To me, of course, she is much more precious now than she was then, and the beauty of her character has far more than made up for the comparative fading of face and form. But I would not be speaking the truth if I did not admit that, physically, time has done its work and left its mark, even as it has with me. That's how it goes in this world, where sin affects everything and everybody. We start out with a lovely face and form and schoolgirl complexion, but time changes all that considerably.

But, in glorious contrast, our Lord started out with a Bride all marred and stained with sin and its dreadful consequences, but when He gets through with His Church, she will be perfect like Himself - spotless and pure, dazzlingly beautiful, within and without. The world will then look at us, and admire Him; see 2 Thess. 1:10.

Praise God for that day, when He shall display His Bride to wondering worlds, and make all to come and worship at her feet (Rev. 3:9), as well as at His feet!

# Christian's Armour

*"Finally, my brethren, be strong in the Lord, and in the power of His might. Put on the whole armour of God, that ye may be able to stand against the wiles of the devil...Stand therefore, having your loins girt about with truth, and having on the breastplate of righteousness; and your feet shod with the preparation of the gospel of peace;*

*"Above all, taking the shield of faith, wherewith ye shall be able to quench all the fiery darts of the wicked. And take the helmet of salvation, and the sword of the Spirit, which is the Word of God: Praying always with all prayer and supplication in the Spirit, and watching thereunto with all perseverance and supplication for all saints."*

(Eph. 6:10-11, 14-18)

The christian life is presented here as a battle. Paul loved to use military figures as he does here, or when he speaks of us as soldiers of Jesus Christ, or when we are told to fight the good fight of faith.

In ordinary fighting, much depends upon the skill and wise guidance of the Commander-in-Chief. In the spiritual life, all depends on Christ, our Captain. In wars between armies, the high officers, seeing they are of such importance, must stay out of danger, and the actual fighting is done by those under their command.

But, in this fight of faith, it is our Commander-in-Chief who went ahead of the armies and gained the victory alone, all by Himself. This is illustrated in David's victory over Goliath. So, Christ met the foe alone and there remains, as it were, only the mopping up to be done; the victory has been won by Him, not by us.

He defeated the enemy at Calvary when He destroyed him that had the power of death, that is, the devil. We are told that He always leads us in the triumph of Christ (2 Cor. 2:14); and that He gives us the victory through our Lord Jesus Christ (1 Cor. 15:57).

As the ark went through the waters of Jordan 2,000 cubits ahead of the people, so our blessed Lord faced all the powers of sin, hell, death and darkness alone and came forth victorious.

The following story is told about General Pershing. After the Armistice, when the Commander-in-Chief had returned to this country, he was royally welcomed, of course, and praised voluminously. At one banquet, after the chairman had lauded the hero with the usual fulsome praise, General Pershing said something like this in reply: "Gentlemen, I must confess that not everybody has such a high opinion of my worth.

"One night during the war, after a very strenuous day, I was taking a walk away behind the lines to rest my mind a little before retiring to rest. Suddenly I heard the footsteps of a man running in my direction. I moved over a few feet, and when he was about to pass me in the thick darkness, I grabbed him by the arm and said: 'Where are you going in such a hurry?'

"He proved to be a soldier from the southern states. 'I'se running away from the front,' said he. 'The bullets are flying thick and fast out there, and I'se apt to get hurt.' 'Yes, I know,' said I, 'but you can't desert like that, you know. That is a capital offence and, if you were caught, you could get shot.' He replied, 'I don't care; I might as well get shot back here as out there; I ain't gwine back!'

"So, to impress him with the seriousness and the peril of his act, I said to him: 'Do you know who this is speaking to you? I am General Pershing, the Commander-in-Chief of all the armies!' The soldier stretched his eyes wide open, exclaiming: 'Land's sakes, yo' all don't mean I'se that far back already!' He did not know he had run that fast."

Yes, those generals had to guard their lives. Our blessed Lord gave His life, in the very forefront of the battle. He is the victorious, risen Lord, and He bids us to enlist in the war that has already been decided. We're just to engage in the mopping-up exercises, though they are real and sanguine enough. We are to take precious souls captive, through the preaching of the gospel, the message of redeeming love.

Satan does not like this and will oppose the work of God with all his might, and so we are to put on the whole armour of God. As has so often been remarked, there was no armour provided for the back. We must never turn our backs to Satan, nor tell Satan to get behind our back.

You have heard the story of the little boy who had been unwisely told by his mother, when he was tempted to do something wrong, to say to the devil: "Get thee behind me, Satan." When next he grievously disobeyed his mother some time later, she said to him: "Didn't I tell you to say, 'Get behind me, Satan'?" "And that's what I did, Mother, and then he pushed me into it!"

Of course, you and I can't trust the devil behind us; the only one who could do so was our Lord Himself, who twice over told Satan just that. We must keep our face to the front, with the armour on and the shield of faith to protect us.

Above and beyond all, we must pray, which is the expression of our need and of our dependence upon His strength, which is so much greater than our own. Not only must we pray for ourselves, but for others; we must engage in supplication for all saints.

When we speak about praying, we do not mean asking for selfish things. Sometimes, almost unconsciously, we are apt to pray in the spirit of the young girl who petitioned: "Lord, I am not asking anything for myself, but please give my mother a son-in-law." When we pray, seeking His glory alone, then we have confidence toward God.

There must be perseverance in prayer, and watching for the answer. Leaving out the selfish purpose, we should pray like the little boy who very much wanted a watch for Christmas.

Day in and day out, in many direct and sometimes subtle ways, he reminded everybody in the house that what he wanted, more than anything else, for Christmas was a watch. Finally, his father told him that if he even once more asked for a watch, he would be sure not to get it, they were so tired of that refrain.

Well, it so happened that, every morning at the breakfast table, each one of the children recited a verse from the Bible from memory. One particular morning, when it came to the watch-conscious boy's turn, he solemnly quoted Mark 13:37: "And what I say unto you, I say unto all, Watch." I don't know whether he got it or not, but he should have.

Pray! Don't give up! Wait for the answer in watchful faith. God loves to honour faith and perseverance.

# Perfect Work in Us

*"Being confident of this very thing, that He which hath begun a good work in you will perform it until the day of Jesus Christ."*

(Phil. 1:6)

A good work was done for us at the Cross by our Lord Jesus Christ. Now, according to the above text, a good work is being done in us by the ministry of the Holy Spirit. The work done for us is a finished work, as John 19:30 assures us; the work in us is not yet complete; it is being carried on.

The verb "perform" is basically the same word Jesus spoke on the Cross, "It is finished"; and, like that word, means "to make perfect". The work in us is being perfected. As Paul says in Philippians 3:12, we are not already perfect. This work in us will reach completion in the day of Jesus Christ. This is the day when the Lord shall come to take His loved Bride home, and we shall be seen as perfect at the Judgment Seat of Christ. Paul again speaks of that day of Jesus Christ in Philippians 1:10 and 2:16.

God began a good work in us when He saved us by His

grace, and He will never be satisfied till that work ends in absolute perfection. God is a perfectionist.

It has been said that an earthly father or mother is so easily pleased, but very difficult to satisfy. Here is a little girl in the home. She is just taking her first wobbling, halting steps, and her parents are watching and encouraging her, with grins on their faces that spread from ear to ear. How pleased they are to see their darling walk for the first time; but those same parents would be grieved beyond words if that child still wobbled five years later. They are pleased with those first stumbling steps, but they will not be satisfied till that little girl becomes a lovely, healthy, intelligent, physically, mentally and morally capable young woman. Even so, our Lord wants to see His saints develop in spiritual growth and usefulness, in moral and spiritual beauty.

God is a God never satisfied, short of perfection. His standards are far higher than ours. Do you remember asking your children, when they were small, whether they had washed their hands before coming to the table? "Oh, yes," said they. "Let's see," said you. "Go right back to the bathroom and wash those dirty wrists and arms. It looks to me as if you washed on the towel and wiped in the water!"

That child's standard of cleanliness is not up to yours. But the doctor maintains a still higher one. He washes his hands before an operation, not once or twice, but several times; he uses soap and antiseptics; he must have absolute cleanliness. Yet his standard is still lower than God's is in the spiritual realm.

God starts His work in us as believers long before we were saved. He started at our natural birth. Paul says that he was separated for the Lord's work from his mother's womb (Gal. 1:15). God has a plan for our lives that is put into operation at our very birth, fitting us for a place later on in His kingdom. Then, He calls us by the gospel, saves us by His grace, and installs the mighty power of the Holy Spirit in us to carry on the work begun in the soul, till that day of perfection has been reached, till we are completely conformed to the image of His Son.

Our God employs various means to perfect the work in us. The most blessed way is by engaging our minds and hearts with Christ, as we read in 2 Corinthians 3:18: "But we all, with open face beholding as in a glass the glory of the Lord, are changed into the same image from glory to glory, even as by the Spirit of the Lord."

And then there is the hard way, by discipline, which we so often need, and is so painful, too. He produces in us likeness to Christ through life's experiences of failure and sin. Our blessed Lord never needed this, because He is and ever was perfect.

When it says in Hebrews 2:10 that the Captain of our salvation was made perfect through sufferings; and in Hebrews 5:9 that, being made perfect, He became the Author of eternal salvation, those passages do not teach that Christ as a "person" was made perfect, but as the Author and Captain of our salvation. Unless He had endured the sufferings of the Cross, He could not have been our Saviour. His perfection as our Saviour depended on His sufferings on the Cross when He bore our sins. In Himself, He was always perfect; we are not, but God is making us so. In dealing with us in discipline and chastisement, He is making us what He wants us to be, and this is often a painful process. 1 Peter 1:7 speaks of this as being tried by fire; and Hebrews 12:11 tells us it is not "joyous, but grievous: nevertheless afterward it yieldeth the peaceable fruit of righteousness unto them which are exercised thereby."

It is something like this: A blacksmith wants to make a certain piece of steel to fit into a certain special spot. He heats it white hot in his forge, and then proceeds to pound it into shape. I frequently used to see this years ago, when I worked in a machine shop. The boss had a small tap hammer in his hand, and his assistant had a great big sledge hammer. The boss would tap lightly, perhaps, on a certain section of the metal, and then the man with the sledge hammer would hit it there. If the boss tapped lightly, it meant that his helper was to strike there rather lightly; if he hit it hard, then the assistant would really let the iron have it. So, between the two of them, the metal would be hammered into the shape needed for the special service it was to perform.

So it is in the christian life. The one with the small hammer pictures God; the one with the big sledge hammer is the devil. Scriptures show that the discipline of the believer is often administered by the devil. Remember how the Lord said to Peter that Satan wanted to get at him to test him, and that the Lord permitted it? Yet, at the same time, Jesus prayed for Simon Peter that his faith might not fail.

A very striking sample of this divine discipline is seen in the case of Job. God permitted Satan to afflict Job, but only by His permission, and he could hit Job only as hard as God let him. God employs Satan to fit and fashion us for His glory, to carry on the process of our ultimate perfection. The whole process is directly under the control of our loving Father. The total result is that we are thus perfected into the very form in which He can use us for Himself, even as the steel is shaped into its desired pattern.

If that iron could talk, it would tell us that the fire burns and the pounding hurts, even as we do know that fiery trials are not pleasant - discipline is not joyous, but grievous. But oh, that blessed afterwards! Even here and now, we get real blessing out of our troubles.

A brother told me once that he was riding on the train and, behind him, sat two old ladies who were, so he said, having an organ recital on the train and seemed to enjoy it immensely. They were talking about all the organs they had taken out in operations, and were getting a real kick out of their reminiscenses.

Did you ever notice, when a group of folks get together chatting, that they talk far more about the troubles they have had in life than over their good times? I believe that, when we get to Glory, we will thank the Lord more for the trials of the way than for anything else.

God seeks our moral perfection, likeness to Christ. Physically, we get worse with the years; spiritually, we should get better. The spiritual development is a process; the physical transformation will take place in one tremendous, climactic moment when Jesus comes to take us Home, for "when we see Him we shall be like Him, for we shall see Him as He is". We shall be changed physically in a moment, praise His Name!

Do not faint under the process. Do not resent it. If you do, God might throw you on the scrapheap as unfit for any real service. Hebrews 12 tells us not to despise this process, nor to faint, but to endure. Our Lord Himself passed through the fire of trial - not to make Him perfect, as in our case, but rather to prove that He was.

We'll be perfect in that day; but some may be a perfect "hut", so to speak, while others will be a perfect "palace". Don't be satisfied with mediocrity; God isn't!

# Thoughts on Philippians

*"Paul and Timotheus, the servants of Jesus Christ, to all the saints in Christ Jesus which are at Philippi, with the bishops and deacons: Grace be unto you, and peace, from God our Father, and from the Lord Jesus Christ. I thank my God upon every remembrance of you, always in every prayer of mine for you all making request with joy."*

(Phil. 1:1-4)

Just a brief introduction to this practical letter to the Philippians, the theme of which is the life of the Christian, patterned after the perfect life of Christ. The prominent theme of the epistle to the Ephesians is the Church here upon the earth, with Christ as her Head in heaven. Colossians presents the exact reverse, with Christ as the Head in heaven the prominent theme, and the Church on earth secondary.

In Philippians, we see Christ prominently in view, both in

heaven and on earth, and the believers with their eyes of faith fixed on Christ in heaven, seeking to live like Christ did when He was on earth. It is all Christ in this letter - a Christ to be manifested by the saints here on earth, in their daily words and works.

The first chapter gives us, as it were, Christ as our life; chapter two, our pattern; chapter three, our goal; and chapter four, Christ our strength. I heard a preacher say once that the four chapters present, also, the following thoughts:

Chapter 1 - the believer captured by Christ.
Chapter 2 - the believer conquered by Christ.
Chapter 3 - the believer captivated by Christ.
Chapter 4 - the believer controlled by Christ.

As you know, the word Philippi means a "lover of horses"; hence it is truly appropriate that this letter so aptly describes the Christian as a racer, running in order to obtain the prize.

The opening verse of this letter to the Philippians presents, as it were, the set-up of the Church, or the assembly, in any given place. We read first of God's servants, then His saints, then of bishops (elders) and deacons.

While in the doctrinal epistles, from Romans through Colossians, Paul introduces himself as the "apostle" of Jesus Christ. Here he is just a servant (bondslave) of Christ, and associates himself with Timothy as such. When it is, therefore, a question of christian living, as in Philippians, Paul comes down to the level of all believers, and takes the lowliest place. He did like his Master, Who took, in marvellous condescension, the form of a slave (chapter 2:7).

Humility becomes the servant of Christ. It is a precious privilege to be a bondslave of Christ. The verse begins with Paul as a slave and ends with saints as deacons, which is also a humble position. Dr. A. T. Robertson says that the Greek word for deacon has the idea of a servant raising dust by being in a hurry to carry out his master's commands. That is the proper place for every believer. There is no room for self-inflation in the service of our Lord.

Paul says, "I magnify mine office" (Rom. 11:13). The trouble with many Christians is that the office magnifies them.

When I was in the Bahamas, one afternoon we anchored in our yacht off a small island. A black man skulled out to us. After a little conversation, we asked him if he would take a supply of tracts ashore with him and give them out to the people. Said he, "Yes, indeed I will. You done give dem tracts to de right man, suh. Ah'll 'stribute them. Do you see that little church up there on the hill? I'se the head sexton of that church!"

I asked him how many more sextons there were, since he was the head one, but found out that he was the only one. He just wanted us to know that he was the head sexton. There are lots of folks occupying offices in religious circles who are about as proud of their position as this black friend was. In contrast, here is this story:

At one time, there was a general in Greece named Epimanondas, who somehow had offended the big shots of that day. So, in order to humiliate him, they appointed him as city scavenger. "Well," said Epimanondas, "if the office does not magnify me, then I'll magnify the office." The tale goes on to say that never in its history did Athens have a clean-up man like Epimanondas. Never was the city so healthful and happy as when he cleaned it and kept it clean. The whole city, in a tribute of appreciation, built a statue to its most honoured and respected citizen - the City Garbage Collector.

Eight times in Philippians, Paul says "you all," so that it has been suggested facetiously that he must have been a Southerner. He, by the Spirit, is speaking to all the saints. Every believer should live for Christ, and should run the race for the prize at the end of the path, no matter where God has been pleased to put him/her; so "you all" get busy!

# Telescope and Microscope

*"According to my earnest expectation and my hope, that in nothing I shall ashamed, but that with all boldness, as always, so now also Christ shall be magnified in my body, whether it be by life, or by death."*

(Phil. 1:20)

*"But we all, with open face beholding as in a glass the glory of the Lord, are changed into the same image from glory to glory, even as by the Spirit of the Lord."*

(2 Cor. 3:18)

I know that the Greek phrase "beholding as in a glass" rather has the idea of looking into a mirror, but I am going to take the liberty of using this expression as implying the idea of looking through a telescope to distant objects. In that way, the two texts above suggest the use of the telescope in 2 Corinthians 3, and the use of the microscope in Philippians 1.

While 2 Corinthians 3:18 does not convey that actual thought, yet it is nevertheless true in Scripture that, by faith, we bring things invisible to the naked eye within the compass of our vision, which is what a telescope does for us.

It is said of Moses that by faith he saw Him who is invisible (Heb. 11:27). Faith brings the unseen God and invisible spiritual realities within our sight.

It has been said of the infidel that he has no invisible means of support. Praise God, neither does a believer, though from a different angle. We do have a support that is invisible to the unbeliever, but not to the Christian.

We see Jesus, crowned with glory and honour. "Faith is the substance of things hoped for; the evidence of things not seen." The Christian uses the telescope of faith and revels in the wonders of God's grace, wisdom and power, which thus become real to his spiritual sight.

A black man was giving evidence in a court case

concerning an auto accident, and was very positive in his statements. Said the lawyer for the defence: "Are you trying to tell this court that you saw all that, and are sure of what you are saying? And all of it on a dark night, too. How far can you see in the night?" Said the witness: "How far is it to the moon?"

He could see that far, and the believer can see infinitely farther - into the very presence of God. Not only can we see farther than that, but some day we shall travel away beyond the moon, into heaven beyond the stars. Even now, like Paul, we can see into the third heaven (by faith, of course), and see and hear unspeakable things, not possible to utter.

Having used the telescope well (the sinner hasn't got one and they are not for sale, though God will make a present of it to every sinner who believes in Jesus), now his body can become the microscope through which the world around can see something of the wonderful things of God. Paul calls his body, as it were, a magnifying glass, a microscope, through which those around him can see (to them, otherwise invisible) the Christ. He wants the Lord Jesus to be magnified in his body: in the life he lived, the words he spoke, the deeds he did, and even in the death he might die.

The worldling cannot see Christ in Glory (the believer can, for he has the telescope of faith), but he can see you and me down here, and should see, in our lives, something that reminds him of Christ. A microscope does not make an object any larger, but it makes it seem bigger and brings it into focus.

So, our blessed Lord cannot be made greater and more wonderful, but in our lives we can bring Him within the vision of the sinner. As Paul said in another connection: "I am crucified with Christ: nevertheless I live; yet not I, but Christ liveth in me: and the life which I now live in the flesh I live by the faith of the Son of God, who loved me, and gave Himself for me" (Gal. 2:20).

As I use the telescope, Christ becomes real to me. As my body (in which I live Christ) is a microscope within the reach of the sinful world around, Christ may become real to those around me. May it be so indeed, for His glory's sake!

# Living and Dying

*"For to me to live is Christ, and to die is gain. But if I live in the flesh, this is the fruit of my labour: yet what I shall choose I wot not. For I am in a strait betwixt two, having a desire to depart, and to be with Christ; which is far better: Nevertheless to abide in the flesh is more needful for you. And having this confidence, I know that I shall abide and continue with you all for your furtherance and joy of faith."*

(Phil. 1:21-23)

To live, and to die (verse 21). They are only a comma apart, and the comma is the punctuation mark suggesting the shortest possible elapse of time. Life and death; the systole and the diastole; the beat and the throb of the pulse; the swing of the pendulum. Every one of us daily stands where this comma stands.

Hamlet weighed the evils of life and the evils of death. He weighed the sorrows of life, from which death could relieve him, over against the terrors of death, from which life as yet delivers him. "To be or not to be", that is the question. Weighing all the evils - the wrongs, the oppressions, the pains, the disappointments of life, he thinks it is better to escape them; but when he considers what unknown death may bring, he turns back to life as preferable. He does not know whether to choose between the wretched present, which is sure, or the perhaps far worse unknown that lies ahead.

Paul was in a dilemma, too, but not for the same reasons. He knew what lay ahead, and it was far, far preferable to the present. Death was no unknown quantity to him. Infinite grace had opened the door of glory to him (as it has to us) and let him look in.

Had he considered himself alone, there would have been no hesitation whatever. To be with Christ was far better, but it was the Lord's people he was thinking of; not himself. They needed him still, he felt, and so he reluctantly turned his back on the inviting prospect of departing to be with Christ and decided to remain here, in this vale of tears, a little longer.

It was not Rome, whose prisoner he was, that decided upon his release from imprisonment; no, the prisoner himself decided his fate. Since the saints needed him a while longer, he was going to live and come back to them, as he tells us in verse 26.

Paul had a problem: to live was Christ; to die was to be with Christ. It was Christ all the way. Mr. Darby is said to have remarked once, when asked how he felt about dying: "There is little to choose between life or death for me. Here Christ is with me; there, I shall be with Christ." So thought Paul.

Paul chooses, and death wins out. It is far better, says he, to die than to live in this world of sin and departure from Him. "Yes," says Paul, "death is far better"; yet...he chooses life. He does not choose the easy path, but the hard one. Love, love for others, depresses the scale in favour of life down below.

How like his Lord, who made the exact same choice. Turn to Luke 9, and you see your precious Lord on the Mount of Transfiguration, clothed in the dazzling beauty and majesty that are His because of who He is. How inviting was the prospect for Him to go back to heaven, as He sees Moses and Elijah return there.

He had a perfect right to do so, but He turned away from it (and only He knows what it cost Him) and went back down to Jerusalem and the awful horror of the Cross. Luke 9:51 tells us that He stedfastly set His face to go to Jerusalem, knowing all that shortly awaited Him there.

Paul, too, chose the suffering of life on earth and a martyr's death, to the infinite joy of heaven. How unlike ourselves usually! We so often want to go to heaven to get away from our trials, not specially because we long to be with Him.

I knew a dear old Christian who really loved the Lord. He

was quite ill for months; and, when feeling real bad, he would say: "Oh, if the Lord would only come to take me home!" But several times, when feeling temporarily much brighter, the first thing he would call for was his pipe. He clung to earth, as most of us do, so don't feel superior. Most of us aren't much better - there are not many Pauls.

But not so Paul. He turned his back on the longed for departure to be with Christ, and remained on earth, with its pains, loneliness and sorrow. So...he decides to abide and continue with the Lord's own. Praise God, the believer does not need to be in a hurry to go to heaven to be with Christ. It is a wonderful privilege to live for Him here below and to suffer for His sake.

During the last world war, it was often very difficult to get seats on trains, since they were so crowded with servicemen, and since many, who otherwise drove their cars, now had to ride the train, due to the shortage of gasoline. I always tried to book passage on a streamliner, and thus get a reserved seat. Otherwise, one would have to come to the station sometimes an hour or more ahead of time and stand in line to get aboard at all, let alone get a seat. With a reserved seat, one did not have to rush or push; the seat was there waiting for you.

So, praise God, we believers do have a reserved seat in heaven. There is no need to be in a rush to get there. It is a very precious privilege, as Paul says, to abide here and to serve the Lord a little longer. We have the honour here of serving where He is rejected, which we shall never have again when we have gone to be with Christ.

"To me to live is Christ" is Paul's motto. Can you and I say that? I can say indeed that "to die is gain", but how about "to live is Christ"? For some believers, to live is seeking wealth; sometimes it is to be somebody; sometimes it is to preach, or to sing, or to write. But to Paul, to live was Christ.

A dear servant of Christ was taken ill, and was told by his physician that his days of active service for Christ were over. His heart would never again permit him to be physically busy. He was confined to his home and oftentimes to his bed. At first, he wished the Lord would take him home, for what good was he since he could not be at the Lord's service, which he had enjoyed so much? But then, one day Philippians 1:21 came to his heart with special force. The verse did not say " to me to live is to preach"; or "to me to live is to comfort the saints and to visit them in their afflictions"; no, "to me to live is Christ". He could still live; and, in living, *Christ* was to be seen in him, and heard, felt, known and enjoyed - not *he*. Let Christ be all, and all will be well!

# Salvation

*"For I know that this shall turn to my salvation through your prayer, and the supply of the Spirit of Jesus Christ."*

(Phil. 1:19)

*"And in nothing terrified by your adversaries: which is to them an evident token of perdition, but to you of salvation, and that of God."*

(Phil. 1:28)

*"Wherefore, my beloved, as ye have always obeyed, not as in my presence only, but now much more in my absence, work out your own salvation with fear and trembling. For it is God which worketh in you both to will and to do of His good pleasure."*

(Phil. 2:12-13)

Salvation is a present possession - 2 Timothy 1:9.
Salvation is a continuous process - Romans 8:10
                           and the Scriptures quoted above.
Salvation is a future accomplishment and fulfillment -
                           Romans 13:11 and Hebrews 9:28.

We might say that the first is past; the second is present; and the third is future.

The first, generally speaking, has to do with the putting away of our sins; the second, with the victory over the dominion of sin within us, so that we may live for His glory; and the third concerns the complete obliteration of sin altogether, when spirit, soul and body shall be made perfect at the coming of the Lord our Saviour.

Or, in other words, salvation is first from the penalty of sin, next from the power of sin, and last, from the presence of sin. The verses quoted for our text refer to this second aspect of salvation. They refer to daily victory in the christian life and testimony for Christ. Paul speaks of salvation in this way as:

my salvation - chapter 1:19
God's salvation - chapter 1:28
your salvation - chapter 2:12.

All three convey the same truth of practical christian living: as this affects Paul's life (or the life of any other believer), as it affects God, and as it affects me.

Believers constantly need to be saved from the dangers, pitfalls and failures due to human weakness which they are heir to. A prominent servant of Christ like Paul would be specially vulnerable to Satanic attacks, and so he greatly valued the prayers of the saints that he might be kept and empowered to serve the Lord and to be kept from the sin and failure which can come so easily.

Their prayers, no doubt, helped in bestowing upon him a special measure of the power of the Spirit. We, too, can thus pray for those in the front line of the battle, that nothing may hinder the utmost degree of usefulness for which God has fitted that particular servant of His. Paul says something similar in 2 Corinthians 1:11.

The believer never needs to be depressed. In spite of opposition and even bitter persecution, God's truth triumphs, impressing the sinner that he is courting perdition, while God vindicates His way and proves, both in the message preached and in the courage and devotion of His messengers, that this salvation is indeed of God (see verse 28).

Every Christian works out the salvation which is said to be "his own" salvation. He works it out in a blameless, pure life, because God, through His Holy Spirit, works in him. God, in the Christian's experience, works from the inside out.

# Concern for Others

*"Let nothing be done through strife or vainglory; but in lowliness of mind let each esteem other better than themselves. Look not every man on his own things, but every man also on the things of others.*

*"Let this mind be in you, which was also in Christ Jesus: who, being in the form of God, thought it not robbery to be equal with God: but made Himself of no reputation, and took upon Him the form of a servant, and was made in the likeness of men:*

*"And being found in fashion as a man, He humbled Himself, and became obedient unto death, even the death of the Cross. Wherefore God also hath highly exalted Him..."*

(Phil. 2:3-9)

It is said that, when the General of the Salvation Army, General Booth, was unable to attend a certain convention, he sent a wire containing only one word to express his attitude towards the service of Christ: "Others".

That word might well describe the theme of the second chapter to the Philippians. "Let each esteem others better than themselves", and "Look not every man on his own things, but every man also on the things of others."

I do not find it difficult to esteem others better than myself, for I know far less about failure and sin in the lives of my fellow believers than I do in my own. I can honestly say with Paul that, in my own sight, I am the least of all saints, and I honour even the feeblest believer, with a deep sense of the great mercy divine grace has shown him.

I take it that, in the fourth verse of this chapter, Paul not only means to be interested in your own service for Christ and concerned for what you spend for His sake, but that you should also show a real interest in what others are doing for Him, with the intent to encourage, cheer and help them.

In order to emphasize his point, the apostle proceeds in this chapter to illustrate it by calling attention to four persons who practised what Paul was now preaching in verses three and four. These four are: the Lord Jesus Himself, Paul, Timotheus, and Epaphroditus.

Who ever saw such an example of absolute surrender of self for the sake of others, as did our holy Lord who, though so rich, for our sakes became poor, that He might make us rich for all eternity? He who was first became last of all.

It reminds me of a story I heard once. A number of patients were waiting in a doctor's office for their turn to be called in, when an excited lady burst into the room and said: "Oh, I wish the person that is next will please let me take his place. I've just got to see the doctor immediately; I simply can't wait!" So, the gentleman next in line acted like a gentleman and, when his call came, he allowed the woman to take his place. When she came forth after a while, with profuse thanks to the man who had given her his turn, that worthy gentleman was about to go in, when there came a vigorous protest from several of the other patients.

"Oh, no," they said, "you can't do that. If you go in now, everyone in the room will lose a turn. We did not give this lady our turn - you did. Since she was last and you made her first, you will now have to sacrifice your first place and take the last one." They were right.

Our blessed Lord did not have to do that; but in infinite grace, in mighty sacrifice, He who is first of all became least of all and last of all, that the last might be first. But, praise His Name, He rose from the dead, where He had taken our place; and so, because of His obedience unto death, He has been given the first place, for God hath highly exalted Him.

But that is in heaven. Here on earth, He took the lowest and last place, setting a pattern for every believer to follow. "Let this mind be in you which was also in Christ Jesus." When He, who is everything, was willing to become nothing, then you and I, who are nothing to begin with, ought not to find it too difficult to continue to be nothing to go on with.

Paul was content to be just the drink offering poured out on the sacrifice and service of the Philippian saints. They presented, as it were, the important offering; he considered himself but the humble outpouring of the wine that would hardly be noticed, but was expressive of the joy he found in the devotion of those saints.

Timothy was far more concerned with the welfare of those saints than with his own. Others often lived for self; he, only for the things that advanced the interests of the Lord Jesus Christ.

Epaphroditus was full of sorrow, not because he was seriously ill (which he was), but because he worried lest they might worry about him. Did you ever hear anything like that before? This dear brother had been sick nigh unto death, not because there was sin in his life, as some folks harshly conclude when a believer is ill, but because he had been neglecting his health in his fervent adherence to the service of his Lord.

A good example of lives lived for others is that of parents for their children, especially a mother. Even in the smallest matters, a mother is so absorbed in her family that she sacrifices constantly for them, without even being aware of it.

I have sometimes remarked that, when we were first married and there were just the two of us, when she baked a pie, my wife and I could each have one half of it, if we wished. We sometimes did, for, praise be, those calories had not been invented yet in those days. When we had one child growing up, this half a pie was reduced to a third. Later, we got only a fourth; and, finally, with four children, our sacrifice of pie had reduced us from a half to a sixth. In fact, my wife often (but not dad, I am ashamed to say) would go without any pie altogether if any of the children happened to want a second helping.

I don't think that dear mother ever thought she was living for others then, but she was in that small way, and in larger ones, too. You are never happy when you live for self. As in the case of a mother, the power to live for others is traced to love. The love of Christ constrains us henceforth not to live unto ourselves, but unto Him who died for us and rose again.

# Perils of Christian Life

*"Finally, my brethren, rejoice in the Lord...Beware of dogs, beware of evil workers, beware of the concision. For we are the circumcision, which worship God in the spirit, and rejoice in Christ Jesus, and have no confidence in the flesh."*

(Phil. 3:1-3)

This wonderful chapter presents the christian life as a race to be run, from the start to the finish, till the coming of the Lord. I'd like to suggest that this chapter shows: the perils, the passion, the purpose, the path, and the prospect of life in and for Christ.

The pistol shot, to start us off in the christian race, is "rejoice in the Lord". In a race, what is needed is endurance, and the "joy of the Lord is your strength". It is not "rejoice in circumstances", which is what the worldling does; nor "rejoice in the truth", which is good and to be craved; but it is even more important than that: it is "rejoice in the Lord". Circumstances chiefly affect the body, and truth the mind, but the Lord fills the heart.

The story is told of a certain Eastern king who was told by one of his courtiers that, if he could wear the shirt of a perfectly happy man, then he would be happy, too. So the king sent couriers all throughout his realm to find a really happy man. Finally, one messenger seemed to have obtained his purpose away back in the mountains. He came across a poor shepherd who bubbled over with happiness. But alas, they were as far from success as ever, for when they asked him for his shirt, it turned out that he was so poor he didn't own one. The moral is that you can be perfectly happy and not even own a shirt; and you can be perfectly unhappy and miserable while owning everything on earth.

I spent part of thirteen years on the water, as we sailed with the gospel throughout the Bahama Islands. I learned in those years that any nitwit almost can handle a sailing vessel when it is blowing a steady easterly breeze and the skies are clear; but it takes a sailor to do so in a heavy storm, or when there is a rage on at the bar.

Even so, anybody can be happy when circumstances are propitious; but only a Christian can rejoice when sorrows, troubles, persecution, etc. come, for the believer's joy is not in things, but in the Lord of things. The believer does not live and do the best under the circumstances, but he lives in the clear sky of God's love, in tune with his Lord, above the circumstances. Things never made folks happy, and Christians sometimes are apt to forget that, as well. In fact, the more you have of earthly goods, the more bothered you often are.

When we were first married, we started out very simply - no fancy furniture, just plain floors, no rugs. But we got up in society, so we bought store furniture and, oh glory, we bought some rugs. Now there was more housecleaning to be done, the rugs wore out, the carpet sweeper got so busy it began to wear out, and bye and bye my wife wore out, wearing out the sweeper! We found that the more we got, the more miseries we got, too. It's not those things that make a home - it is love, that sacrifices and suffers and rejoices, that makes a home. It was our joy in each other that made life worth living.

The greatest joy of all is the joy we have "in the Lord". We are urged to rejoice in the Lord, for that gives us spiritual strength and stamina, and we need this in order to meet the perils that confront us.

There are three things in verse 2:

Dogs - Evil Workers - the Concision.

Beware of dogs! This is a term applied in Scripture to those outside. In the case of the Jews - the Gentiles; in general, referring to those unsaved, who belong to this world. Believers are warned against being infected with the spirit of the world.

When it tells us to beware of dogs, it does not have their tails in view, of course, but their mouths; it is their bite that constitutes the danger. The bite of a dog is apt to induce hydrophobia, which means the "fear of water". An animal afflicted with this terrible scourge of hydrophobia fears water while, at the same time, craving it, so I understand.

It is thus the disease that may well mark the sinner. He has a thirst which only God can satisfy, yet, at the same time, he turns away from the only water that can satisfy that thirst, the water of life that the Lord Jesus spoke of to that woman in John 4:13-14.

A Christian, bitten by a dog affected by contact with the world, will suffer the same symptoms. He, too, will turn from the water of life, God's Word. One of the first proofs a Christian is away from God is his loss of appetite for God's Word. So, beware of dogs!

Beware of evil workers! This does not have in view mere unbelievers, as the word "dogs" does, but those who teach and believe false doctrines. Paul calls them false apostles, deceitful workers (which agrees with the term "evil workers" in our text) in 2 Corinthians 11:13, where the evident thought is that of teaching devilish falsehoods.

The Christian is here warned, then, against listening to false doctrines. Satan usually does not come right out with his evil lies and, in that way, deceives believers not well acquainted with the Word of God. That's why John (see John 2:9-10) bids us to listen not to what such say, but to what they do not say. He warns against those who bring not the true doctrine. In other words, if you hear anyone speak, and they do not clearly show their faith is in Christ as the Son of God, nor do they mention the worth of His precious blood, you may know they are false - the tools of Satan.

One Sunday, during the last world war, my older son, Elliot, and I were in Montgomery, Alabama, where he was stationed. Not knowing anyone there, we chose a certain church from the newspaper advertisements, and went there. When we came out, my son said to me: "Dad, a Mohammedan, a Hindu, a Hottentot, a Buddhist, an infidel and others could all have enjoyed that sermon in this so-called christian church, except a Christian."

That preacher did not say anything wicked; he just did not say anything. He never once mentioned the name of Christ, except at the end of his closing prayer. It is not the evil he said (he said none), but the truth he left out that marked him as an evil worker.

Mr. Spurgeon said once, so I hear, that if a baker sold you a loaf of bread made of sawdust, never buy another loaf in that store. The Lord said, "Beware of false prophets which come to you in sheep's clothing." How do you know whether a preacher is a sheep or a wolf? Not by how he looks, for the Lord had just told us that false prophets are dressed like sheep. You find out, not by looking at their lives, but by listening to their words. For when a wolf, even though dressed like a sheep, opens its mouth, you'll hear that it can't say "baa baa" like a sheep; instead, it will growl.

In order to beware of false liars, you don't have to read up on every theory they advance, or every voice that clamours for attention, either from the pulpit or at your house door. All you need is to be acquainted with the Word of God, which is truth. Then, you'll instantly detect the counterfeit when it comes along. You don't swallow poison to find out if it is poison; it is wiser and safer to go by the label on the bottle. "My sheep hear My voice," says our blessed Lord.

One night, on a stormy lake, the Saviour spoke peace to His storm-tossed disciples, saying: "Be of good cheer; it is I; be not afraid." He did not say, "This is Jesus"; just "It is I".

Now, who is "I", anyway? This same experience has come to all of us often. Late at night, the door bell rings at my home, and when I ask, "Who is there?" the answer comes, "It's me" (ungrammatical, but graphic). Now, who on earth is "me"? There are about 3000 million "me's" in this world. How do I know which "me" this one is? I know it, of course, by the tone of the voice. If it is the voice of one close and dear to me, how sweet that voice sounds! The better I know that voice, the more I have heard it, the more sure I am of the identity of that person, and the less danger there is of admitting an evil person into my home.

Even so said Jesus: "My sheep hear My voice." The more you listen to the voice of Christ (through God's Word), the less danger there is of your being deceived by Satanic falsehoods. Hear Him often. Feed on God's Word every day, and the devil will not make a dope or a dupe out of you.

Beware of the concision. In the case of dogs, it is the world the Christian is bidden to beware of. In the case of evil workers, it is the devil to be guarded against; and finally, it is the flesh - the three great traditional enemies of the believer in Jesus.

Paul contrasts concision with circumcision. Circumcision applies spiritually to the complete cutting off of the flesh with its lusts. Concision is a cheap imitation, implying only the cutting off of pieces, so to speak, while keeping the flesh itself as something to expect good from. It implies cutting off the branches, while leaving the tree whole. It suggests that I myself am not so bad, though I may do wrong things.

But the true christian attitude is that man himself is totally corrupt - that in me, in my flesh, dwells no good thing. That henceforth I live; yet not I, but Christ lives in me. Concision implies confidence in self; circumcision implies no trust in self at all, but trust altogether and alone in Christ, with a deep sense of our own utter sinfulness and helplessness.

Peter is a good example of the concision we are to beware of. You remember that Gideon won a mighty battle with 300 men, who carried torch lights within their pitchers, and who, on a given signal, smashed their pitchers so that the light could shine forth. Simon Peter had a pitcher, too, with the light of God's salvation on the inside. But Peter thought too much of his pitcher to smash it - he loved its beauty and worth.

"All those others," said Peter, "may forsake and deny Thee, but not I. Their pitchers probably have flaws, and they might as well smash them, but not mine. Mine is pretty and really too good to break. I'm just going to take the light out, but leave the pitcher whole."

He did take the light out in Matthew 16:16, when he acknowledged Jesus as the Christ, the Son of the living God; but he left it in when, with curses and oaths, he denied his Lord. Not a soul could have known that night that he carried any light at all, for his soul was in total darkness, and he left those around him in the dark, too. He was no victor that night, as Gideon was when he smashed his pitcher, but only a poor, defeated weakling.

Until the flesh is totally broken to slivers, the light will not shine consistently from a believer's life. Only a realization of one's total nothingness in self will make Christ everything in and through the believer.

So, in the second verse of our text, there is a warning against:

Worldliness - in the bite of dogs
Wickedness - in the lies of Satan's emissaries
Worthlessness - in concision, a self-centred life.
No. 1 - Danger lies in aversion to the Word of God.
No. 2 - Danger lies in perversion of the Word of God.
No. 3 - Danger lies in reversion to self.

# Spiritual Reckoning

*"But what things were gain to me, those I counted loss for Christ. Yea doubtless, and I count all things but loss for the excellency of the knowledge of Christ Jesus my Lord: for whom I have suffered the loss of all things, and do count them but dung, that I may win Christ,*

*"And be found in Him, not having mine own righteousness, which is of the law, but that which is through the faith of Christ, the righteousness which is of God by faith."*

(Phil. 3:7-9)

Paul strikes a balance here between profit and loss. The loss of all things is nothing compared with the gain in having Christ. What are things in comparison with the supreme excellence of Christ Jesus our Lord? He was glad, furthermore, to lose himself and to be found again in Christ. His passion was to know Christ, to win Christ, and to be in Christ.

He "counted" - verse 7; he "counts" - verse 8. Perhaps 25 or more years had passed between those two reckonings. When he counted all things loss for Christ at his conversion, no doubt many said that this was only the rash enthusiasm of reckless youth - he'd soon get over it and change his mind. But many years have passed and, after years of suffering, abuse, persecution, heartaches and pain, Paul is still of the same mind. He still counts it a wonderful bargain to have exchanged Christ for all the things he once was so proud of.

He had much to surrender for Christ, but he counts it all dung, and it is not hard to give up garbage. He had seen Christ, and ever after could see none and nothing else. It is said of the fanatic pilgrims to Mecca that sometimes, having looked upon their holy city, they burn their eyes out with hot burning stones, so that never again shall they look on ordinary scenes. Paul could say:

I have heard the voice of Jesus;
Tell me not of aught beside;
I have seen the face of Jesus,
And my heart is satisfied.

The knowledge of Christ is supreme in excellence. There are agnostics, there are gnostics, and there are supergnostics. The last are those who know Christ as Lord. The knowledge of Him is superknowledge because it is not the product of reasoning, nor the accumulation of evidence, but a moral conviction, a soul experience, for it is of God, divine, eternal. It is not knowing about God; it is knowing Him.

In mere secular knowledge, the truly healthy result is a realization of one's own nothingness. As one professor put it, "The true benefit derived from a college education is the passage from a state of unconscious ignorance to a state of conscious ignorance," which is, after all, a negative effect, stressing what you don't know.

The excellency of the knowledge of Christ is that it produces positive results. It first teaches you your own insignificance, but also His infinite worth. I saw a statement once, in that line, which impressed me. It said: "The more upright a sinner is, the less conscious he is of his imperfections; but the more upright a Christian is, the more he is conscious of his own shortcomings, for in closer walking with his Lord, he sees how far short he comes of the absolute beauty and glory that shine forth in Him."

Yet, at the same time, his character is shaped after the pattern of Christ's perfection, for unconsciously he will imitate the One with whom he walks in communion. The excellence of the knowledge of Christ is that it changes character and makes the believer more Christlike, while academic knowledge never does. Often the most erudite are at once the most immoral.

In the presence of Christ, we learn two salutary lessons. Job illustrates the one, and the once-blind man of John 9 the other. Both of these men had been blind and had gotten their eyes opened. Both first heard and then saw the Lord, and it produced revolutionary changes in both cases.

Job had been spiritually blind, as he confesses when he says: "I have heard of Thee by the hearing of the ear: but now mine eyes seeth Thee; Wherefore I abhor myself, and repent in dust and ashes" (Job 42:5-6).

The man in John 9 had been both physically and spiritually blind, and illustrates in his experience the conversion of a soul.

In answer to Jesus' question, "Dost thou believe on the Son of God?" he replied, "Who is He, Lord, that I might believe on Him?" Jesus said to him, "Thou hast both seen Him and it is He that talketh with thee." The blind man answered, "Lord, I believe," and he worshipped Him. Like Job, this blind man had heard the Lord's voice before he saw His face.

Hearing and seeing are two different things. The sinner first hears the Word of God and then, by faith, sees the One who is its theme; thus, the heart is won. In Job's case, it led to abhorrence of self; in the blind man's case, to adoration of the Saviour.

That's where the knowledge of Christ is super-excellent, as Philippians 3:8 indicates, because it not only makes one realize one's own sin and failure, but, filling the heart and mind with His grace and glory, it results in a loathing of self and a lauding of the Lord Jesus, and this results in a moral conformity to Christ.

# Knowing Christ

*"That I may know Him, and the power of His resurrection, and the fellowship of His sufferings, being made conformable unto His death."*

(Phil. 3:10)

Paul's great desire was to know Christ, which is the height of christian attainment. He says this after having known Christ for many years. He thus confesses, as it were, that he feels he did not know Him at all yet, though perhaps no saint ever knew Him more intimately than Paul did. For us, then, "there remaineth yet very much land to be possessed". To know Him, in three outstanding ways:

1. the power of His resurrection,
2. the fellowship of His sufferings,
3. conformity to His death.

Chronologically, Christ's resurrection comes last of the three features here given. So, since it is placed first, it intimates that Paul is thinking of His resurrection as its truth affects us. We do not live at all until we have experienced resurrection.

By faith, we are risen with Christ (Col. 3:1), and raised from the death of sin, we now have and live eternal life (John 5:24). I take it, then, that Paul wanted to know the power of a resurrected life, a resurrection that puts us as believers in a new sphere, no longer of the world, though still in the world; living in, yet living above the world.

The fellowship of His sufferings next tells the story that, though we live in touch with heaven, yet in body we are still on earth, and so have the privilege of sharing in His sufferings. It speaks not of His sufferings at the hand of God when He bore our sins on the Cross (which, praise His Name, we shall never know); but the sufferings He endured at the hands of men during His life on earth. Not many believers can honestly say that they crave to know those sufferings, but Paul did.

He was set as a pattern of longsuffering to those who were to come after him (see 1 Timothy 1:16).

"Being made conformable unto His death." The death of Christ bespeaks total self-abnegation. He died entirely for others; yea, first of all for God. God is glorified in His death, and man is blessed. Paul would know that in his own experience - a complete self-emptying, as seen in our Lord's own exemplary death (see Phil. 2:7).

This precious ambition of Paul concerns:

God, as in newness of life, he now lives unto Him;

self, as he shares in the reproach and sufferings of Christ;

others, as his life is spent to save sinners and bless saints.


# Paul's Path


*"That I may know Him, and the power of His resurrection, and the fellowship of His sufferings, being made conformable unto His death; if by any means I might attain unto the resurrection of the dead.*

*"Not as though I had already attained, either were already perfect: but I follow after, if that I may apprehend that for which also I am apprehended of Christ Jesus.*

*"Brethren, I count not myself to have apprehended: but this one thing I do, forgetting those things which are behind, and reaching forth unto those things which are before, I press toward the mark for the prize of the high calling of God in Christ Jesus.*

*"Let us therefore, as many as be perfect, be thus minded: and if in any thing ye be otherwise minded, God shall*

*reveal even this unto you. Nevertheless, whereto we have already attained, let us walk by the same rule, let us mind the same thing."*

(Phil. 3:10-16)

Here we have Paul's path. Let's look at a few highlights. In verse 12 Paul says that he is not yet perfect; yet in verse 13 he says that he is. This involves no contradiction. He is speaking of perfection of attainment in verse 12; and of perfection of purpose or ambition in verse 15. He is in dead earnest. He pursues, verse 12; reaches forth, verse 13; presses on, verse 14; follows after, verse 17; and weeps in verse 18. Most of these activities can't be done while sitting in a rocking chair.

Paul does "one" thing. Like a racer, he fixes his eye upon the goal and presses on in order to win the prize. A man running a race cannot afford to look behind him or to look around.

When we were boys, we'd sometimes race with each other through the snow. The mark would be a distant tree, and we'd each start running from a different spot. The idea was to get to the tree first, and the fastest, but to make a straight track while doing so. Boy-like, one might turn around to see how he was doing, or would look at the other boys to see if they were beating him. Each time he did so, he'd make a crook in his own track through the snow. It is so in the christian life. To make straight paths for your feet, you must keep your eye of faith fixed on Christ.

Paul forgot the things behind and reached out after those lying before him. Man was built to look forward and to go forward. I understand the very meaning of the Greek word for man, "anthropos", has the thought of eyes and face forward.

God has given us eyes only in the front of our heads. (With the tremendous traffic on the roads today, a pair behind might come in very handy!) Our knees bend forward instead of backward, as with most animals. Our ears are slanted forward, also, and the nose is forward, too, sometimes making men too nosey. Man's construction is a parable, and the Christian especially needs to recognize this.

Forget the past and reach out to the future. Old folks often love to look back and reminisce, but believers strong in spiritual health must press on. I don't think Paul was having his sins in mind when he spoke of forgetting the things behind. He did that in verses 4-7 of this chapter. In verse 13 he is speaking of his life as a believer; of his accomplishments in the service of Christ. He does not look back to what has been done for Christ, but rather to what may still be done.

He would live the remainder of his life actively pursuing the calling to which the Lord had called him. Like the old mountaineer laconically said, when asked by a passerby if he had lived in those hills all his life, "Not yet." Neither have you and I finished our course yet; let's get on with it!

The prize? "The high calling of God in Christ Jesus." I think the thought here is that of Luke 14:10, where the Lord suggests that those who take a low place here will be called up higher in the day of reward. The Lord will call such up high, as in our text. Paul envisages that day when, in the presence of multitudes in the glory above, he shall be called higher, to be honoured in the sight of millions for his devotedness to Christ down here.

# The Cross and the Believer

*"Brethren, be followers together of me, and mark them which walk so as ye have us for an ensample. (For many walk, of whom I have told you often, and now tell you even weeping, that they are the enemies of the cross of Christ: whose end is destruction, whose God is their belly, and whose glory is in their shame, who mind earthly things.)*

*"For our conversation is in heaven; from whence also we look for the Saviour, the Lord Jesus Christ: who shall change our vile body, that it may be fashioned like unto His glorious body, according to the working whereby He is able even to subdue all things unto Himself."*

(Phil. 3:17-21)

Some were enemies of the Cross of Christ, and it made Paul weep. It does not say they were enemies of Christ, but of His cross. The Cross suggests the painful part of being a Christian. Many are willing to accept and rejoice in what Christ did to put away their sins, but don't relish what the Cross did to put them away. The Cross of Christ is the end of self, as the death of Christ is the end of my sins.

So reads Romans 6:6: "our old man is crucified with Christ". All that I once was is forever set aside as worthless when I take Christ as my Saviour. "I am crucified with Christ" (Gal. 2:20). Proud, upstanding "I" is crossed out at the Cross of Christ. "They that are Christ's have crucified the flesh with its affections and lusts" (Gal. 5:24). "God forbid that I should glory save in the Cross of our Lord Jesus Christ, by whom the world is crucified unto me and I unto the world" (Gal. 6:14).

Shortly after I got saved, the foreman where I worked asked me to go to a show with him (as I had done beforehand a few times). I told him that I would not be able to go for two reasons: (1) I was saved by the grace of God; and (2) it happened to be our prayer meeting night. A few weeks later, he asked me again, and this time I replied again in the negative, and added that I could not go anyway because that night was our weekly Bible Study at the chapel.

He looked me up and down a few times and said, with heavy sarcasm: "Prayer meeting and Bible Study; Prayer meeting and Bible Study; man, you're dead to the world and don't know it."

"Thanks," said I, "you couldn't have said it any better if you had been the apostle Paul, for that's just what he says in Galatians 6:14. He says I am crucified with Christ to the world, and that certainly makes me dead. Only, you said that I didn't know I was dead. You're wrong there. Praise the Lord, I know it a little, at least."

Four things are said of the enemies of the Cross of Christ: (1) their end is destruction; (2) their god is their belly; (3) their glory is in their shame; and (4) they mind earthly things. Now, I thank God that the exact opposite may be true of those who know and love the Lord Jesus. In normal Christianity, the results are the reverse:

Our end is not destruction, but eternal life with Christ in heaven, and reward for faithful service rendered. If man's god is his belly, it is because all he ever thinks about is "taking in"; he lives to gratify self. But, from the belly of the believer, instead of taking in, there flows forth a river of living water, to bring refreshment to thirsty souls, see John 7:38-39. We glory in Him, and not in our shame. We glory in the Cross, because from it streams the more abundant grace of God. Instead of minding earthly things, the believer sets his mind on things above, where Christ sitteth on the right hand of God (Col. 3:1-2).

But, I wonder whether we may not apply this verse 19 to believers as well, for sometimes, alas, there is a grievous lack of vital christian living even in the child of God. His end, too, might be destruction. The same word is translated waste when Judas criticised the pouring of the ointment on Jesus' feet. It says of the steward in Luke 16 that he had wasted his master's goods, even as the prodigal in chapter 15 had wasted his father's goods. The one pictures a sinner; the other a believer.

Believers may waste the goods committed to them as good stewards of the manifold grace of God. In the end, at the Judgment Seat of Christ, their lives may prove to have been largely a waste. Such a believer will suffer loss, though saved himself so as by fire. Their god is their belly. We, too, may take in, yet give out so little. We may listen to God's Word, in a way enjoy it, but return so little to God in the way of worship, service or sacrifice.

Their glory is in their shame. We may pride ourselves on our knowledge or station in life or ecclesiastical position. All glorying in anything but the matchless grace of God is equivalent to glorying in our shame.

They mind earthly things. Isn't that often true as well of real believers? If not, why are we so often urged in Scripture to look up, to look off unto Jesus, to look at the things which are not seen? How much time do we really spend engaged with heavenly things?

"Our citizenship is in heaven; from whence also we look for the Saviour, the Lord Jesus Christ: who shall change our body of humiliation, that it may be fashioned like unto His own body of glory" (Phil. 3:20-21). That word "vile" in our text means humble or low. The exact same word is found in Luke 1:48, where Mary speaks of her low estate. Compared with the body of dazzling beauty we shall have some day, how humble is our present one: limited to earth and, because of sin, often painful, even ugly, twisted, weak, and growing emaciated with the years.

Oh, what a thrill to say goodbye to it forever some day, and to exchange it for a body of unlimited capacity and beauty, with all the marks of sin gone, suited to the glory of God! We are waiting for that event. Our Saviour has not saved us completely as yet. He has saved our soul; He is saving us day by day (Heb. 7:25); and He will finish the work when He gives us our body of perfection at His coming. Glory to His Name!

# Peace of Soul and Mind

*"Let your moderation be known unto all men. The Lord is at hand. Be careful for nothing; but in every thing by prayer and supplication with thanksgiving let your requests be made known unto God. And the peace of God, which passeth all understanding, shall keep your hearts and minds through Christ Jesus."*

(Phil. 4:5-7)

Let your moderation (or yieldedness) be known unto men; let your requests be made known unto God. Don't insist on having your own way in dealing with others, and God will let you have His way.

Be careful for nothing.
Be prayerful in everything.
Be thankful for anything.

This is the Divine Psychiatrist's prescription for a healthy state of soul and mind. Practise this faithfully and you will never have to lie on a couch in a psychiatrist's office. It will prove a remedy better, and certainly cheaper, than the other.

The peace of God will, like a garrison of soldiers, keep the enemy of your soul on the outside, while giving perfect peace and serenity within, for the peace of God shall garrison your hearts and minds through Christ Jesus. Note that the heart is mentioned first. With the heart fixed on Christ, the mind will be kept untroubled.

The peace of God will keep the enemy out, and the God of peace Himself will dwell within. What more could you want?

Elisha prayed for his servant: "Lord, I pray Thee, open his eyes that he may see." And the Lord opened the eyes of the young man, and behold, the mountain was full of horses and chariots of fire round about Elisha. We might well pray for the opened eyes of faith to see the mighty protecting host of the peace of God encompassing us, which keeps us in perfect peace, with the mind stayed on Him.

Don't forget the thanksgiving. Thanks for past mercies which so often we are apt to neglect; and thanksgiving for the things we ask for, even before we receive them. We may not have much we can give to God or man; but one thing we can give, which costs us nothing and yet is oft appreciated more than anything else, is our thanks.

Ten thousand, thousand precious gifts
Our daily thanks employ;
Nor is the least a cheerful heart
To taste those gifts with joy.

# Spiritual Investment

*"Now ye Philippians know also, that in the beginning of the gospel, when I departed from Macedonia, no church communicated with me as concerning giving and receiving, but ye only.*

*"For even in Thessalonica ye sent once and again unto my necessity. Not because I desire a gift: but I desire fruit that may abound to your account.*

*"But I have all, and abound: I am full, having received of Epaphroditus the things which were sent from you, an odour of a sweet smell, a sacrifice acceptable, wellpleasing to God.*

*"But my God shall supply all your need according to His riches in glory by Christ Jesus."*

(Phil. 4:15-19)

Paul was in business for and with Christ, and, as such, he welcomed the fellowship and partnership of the saints. The Philippians had opened an account with Paul, see verse 17; they were in business with him and had become his partners, verse 15; in the biggest enterprise in the world - that of winning souls to Christ.

I heard a dear old brother, with whom I conducted tent meetings almost half a century ago, tell frequently of this experience: He was riding the train through the beautiful Pennsylvania hills when, at a small town, a salesman got on and came and sat next to the preacher. Making conversation, he said: "What a hopeless place that is; I just couldn't do any business there. I'm an insurance salesman, you know." Turning to the preacher, he said: "And what line are you in, sir?"

"Well," said my friend, "strange to say, I am in the insurance business myself, and work for the biggest company in the world." "Metropolitan Life Insurance, eh?" "Oh, no, much bigger than that!" "Can't be," said the salesman, "the Metropolitan is the largest in our line."

The preacher continued: "Nevertheless, the company I work for is much bigger, and it is a most peculiar concern. All the premiums have been paid, the insured one comes in for all the benefits and it does not cost him a penny; and, besides that, it furnishes him fire as well as life insurance, and a limited theft, accident and storm insurance as well."

"What an outfit! I'd like to take out a policy in that company, though I don't see how they can operate and make money that way. How can I get insured with your firm?"

"Very simply," answered the preacher, "just put in your application as a poor guilty sinner, cast yourself on the mercy of God in Christ Jesus, who died for you, and God insures you for eternal life. He guarantees that you'll never lose yourself or your property in the fire of His judgment, and even protects you from thieves so that you can lay up your treasures in heaven.

"The reason why my firm, composed of Father, Son and Holy Spirit, can operate so cheaply is that all the costs have been paid by God's beloved Son upon the Cross. God does not need money. He is fabulously rich and loves to make poor lost sinners rich for all eternity."

I never heard for sure whether this insurance salesman got insured with God or not, but I know you ought to, if still uninsured.

Paul was in that glorious business of divine life and fire insurance. He thanks God that the Philippians had not pulled out of the firm, but were still investing again and again in this tremendous project, see verse 16. He was not interested because of personal advantage to himself; it was not that he desired a gift, but he was anxious to have them get interest from their investment, which he calls (verse 17) fruit to their account. Are we in business with others who are in partnership with the Lord?

On the way home from a missionary rally, a young girl told her mother that somehow she could never get enthusiastic about mission work. At that moment, they happened to be passing a bank. The mother, pointing to the building, said to her daughter: "Yes, I understand you perfectly. You have no interest in the work of the Lord for the same reason you don't have any interest in this bank. It's because you have no account there. The moment you deposit money in the bank, you begin to get interest. Even so, when you put something into the work of saving souls, whether it be your time, talents or your money, you will find that you have interest in it, too." The Philippians did, and so they were interested, and Paul tells them that their investment was producing profits.

You have heard the story of the Scotchman, haven't you? With his week's wages, two golden sovereigns, in his pocket, he went to the missionary meeting one night. The missionary spoke so glowingly about the work of the Lord in his field, and the great need existing, that the Scotchman resurrected those two gold pieces and put one of them in the plate when it passed.

But then, on the way home, he said to himself: "Now I know my wife will really let me have it! She isn't a Christian, and she will think I am crazy for giving half a week's wages to the cause." Sure enough, his anticipation was more than matched by the realization. She did give him a piece of her mind. Not only then, but for weeks afterwards, she would bring it up again and berate him.

About a year later, an uncle of his died in Australia and left him a legacy of one hundred pounds. When he received the cheque from the lawyer's office, the delighted Scotchman waved it triumphantly and said to his wife: "You see, woman, the Lord says in His Word that, if you give to Him, you will receive a hundredfold. I put one pound in the collection, and He has given me one hundred pounds in return."

But you know what that cantankerous old woman said? "Yes, but you didn't believe that when you put that sovereign in the plate, or you would've put them both in!"

The Philippians were liberal givers and Paul assures them of rich returns. God has fabulous riches in glory (verse 19), and He will supply all their need from that exhaustless storehouse of spiritual wealth. He is no man's debtor. I don't think Paul is speaking of the supply of their physical or material needs, but rather how God will bless the soul richly with spiritual joy and power in exchange for the material gifts that His people present to Him.

In verse 18 Paul sends the saints a receipt for their investment. He acknowledges their gift and tells them how abundantly it met the need. He assures them this is no coldblooded business transaction. His letter is no cold, perfunctory financial statement of account, nor is their gift of that order. He says it is a sacrifice of a sweet smell, an odour acceptable, wellpleasing to God.

God's grace adds sweetest perfume to every little act of love for Christ, and thus makes it a valuable contribution to the firm of Father, Son and Holy Spirit. All the glory is to God, verse 20; all the blessing is to the saints, verse 23.

What blessed results flow from devotion to Christ! Note that the saints' investment with Paul:

(1) relieved Paul's need;
(2) gladdened his heart;
(3) enriched the givers; and
(4) brought pleasure to God.

# Hope; Knowledge; Love

*"We give thanks to God and the Father of our Lord Jesus Christ, praying always for you, since we heard of your faith in Christ Jesus, and of the love which ye have to all the saints,*

*"For the hope which is laid up for you in heaven, whereof ye heard before in the word of the truth of the gospel; which is come unto you, as it is in all the world; and bringeth forth fruit, as it doth also in you, since the day ye heard of it, and knew the grace of God in truth:*

*"As ye also learned of Epaphras our dear fellowservant, who is for you a faithful minister of Christ; who also declared unto us your love in the Spirit..."*

(Col. 1:3-8)

I would like to note three prominent thoughts in this passage, involved in the words: hope, verse 5; knowledge, verse 6, and love, verse 8.

HOPE. What a great word in the Bible! In normal life, often proving a severe disappointment, as many a young lady, who prepared her "hope chest", has learned. But "hope" in Scripture does not merely express a desire or wish, but implies positive assurance. In this chapter, we read of hope in heaven, verse 5; hope under heaven, verse 23; and hope in us, verse 27.

The hope of the believer is called a good hope in 2 Thessalonians 2:16; a blessed hope in Titus 2:13; a rejoicing hope in Hebrews 3:6; an assuring hope in Hebrews 6:11, and a living hope in 1 Peter 1:3.

KNOWLEDGE. Agnostics pride themselves on the fact that they know nothing, a rather dubious distinction. Gnostics claim to know, and then Paul speaks of believers in Jesus as those who know fully; we might call them superknowalls.

This knowledge is acquired by the humble believer the very day he hears the gospel by faith and comes to Christ -

the first time he heard the grace of God truly. Into this secret society of the saints, you are initiated by God Himself, upon faith in Christ. You initially learn to know divine things because the Holy Spirit, who knows everything, comes to indwell the soul, see 1 John 2:20.

Note that it says that a soul receives the grace of God in truth. Grace comes first; then truth, for grace and truth came by Jesus Christ (John 1:17). Grace makes its appeal to our sin and need, which is the first requisite. It may not satisfy our reasoning powers because, when we are saved, our thoughts are twisted and warped through sin; we can't think straight. But the love of God can and does reach our hearts.

We had a street meeting in the city of Detroit some forty years ago. A communist kept interrupting us, and we asked him to please behave himself till we were through, and then we would be glad to talk with him.

So, afterwards we listened for some time to his harangue, and finally said to him: "Now you have told us what you think, and we have listened to your reasonings, but where are you? You are still a sinner with a heart full of hatred against God. Now listen for a minute to God's voice, and you'll get somewhere.

"He says, 'Come now, and let us reason together: though your sins be as scarlet, they shall be as white as snow; though they be red like crimson, they shall be as wool' (Isa. 1:18). You see, if you listen to God's reasoning, you'll be pure and holy; but your own reasoning leaves you a dirty, sinful soul."

Superknowledge consists of an experience of the grace of God that saves the soul from sin, followed by an increasing knowledge of the ways and will of God as found in the Word of God, enlightening the mind and purifying the life. This, in turn, will result in a knowledge of His will in all wisdom and spiritual understanding, verse 9.

No believer can transfer this secret, known only to those initiated into the society of the redeemed. I can't tell you; you must come to Christ for yourself, then you'll know. You have heard it said that a woman can't keep a secret; well, I can't tell this secret. "If any man willeth to do His (God's) will," said the Lord, "he shall know of the doctrine" (John 7:17). "The natural man receiveth not the things of the Spirit of God: for they are foolishness unto him: neither can he know them" (1 Cor. 2:14).

LOVE. The unique thing about this verse is that the Holy Spirit is mentioned (being found only once in Colossians), and that He is mentioned in connection with "love", referring to our love for others.

In this letter the Spirit of God, as it were, hides Himself, that the Lord Jesus may be seen. Christ is the "Soloist" on life's stage in the Epistle to the Colossians. The spotlight is focused on Him. Even the Spirit removes Himself, and certainly every mere believer is to get off the stage, that in all things Christ may have the preeminence.

Colossians is the epistle of hidden things. The Spirit hides Himself; the mystery of the Church has been hid from ages and generations, verse 26, and though manifest to saints, is still a hidden mystery to the world. All the treasures of wisdom and knowledge are hid in Christ, chapter 2:3; and our life is hid with Christ in God, chapter 3:3. In all these, Christ alone is to be seen, and believers who truly know Christ will know the wondrous truths found in Him, and will delight to speak of them to each other.

# Know, Go, and Grow

*"For this cause we also, since the day we heard it, do not cease to pray for you, and to desire that ye might be filled with the knowledge of His will in all wisdom and spiritual understanding; that ye might walk worthy of the Lord unto all pleasing, being fruitful in every good work, and increasing in the knowledge of God;*

*"Strengthened with all might, according to His glorious power, unto all patience and longsuffering with joyfulness; giving thanks unto the Father, which hath made us meet to be partakers of the inheritance of the saints in light:*

*"Who hath delivered us from the power of darkness, and hath translated us into the kingdom of His dear Son: in whom we have redemption through His blood, even the forgiveness of sins."*

(Col. 1:9-14)

Paul looks down from the height of glory where the grace of God had raised him, down to the fearsome depths from whence he came. But it makes me dizzy to look down, so I'll start at the bottom and take a look upward. I, too, came from the deep darkness which had blinded my eyes, 1 John 2:11. Such blindness is truly awful. When the light blinds one, it usually is only temporary; but habitual darkness, when the eyes are not being used at all, often results in fatal and hopeless blindness.

They say that when mules were used to draw carts down in coal mines, they eventually became totally blind, because in the profound blackness down there, they had no way to use their eyes, so lost the use of them altogether.

Even so, many sinners live so habitually and wilfully away from the light of God's Word that at last they lose the ability to see at all. How wondrous the love that has brought so many of us out of the darkness into the life-giving light of His Word! The believer is a new translation; he is no longer the old unauthorised version; or, if authorised, only by the authority of the price of darkness; but now he is a revised version, translated into the light, so that others may read Christ in him.

In the past - in the darkness; but now - in the light! In the present, I am in the kingdom of the Son of God's love, to walk worthy of that kingdom, with the blessed assurance that, in the future, I shall be a member of the society of the saints, and shall enjoy the inheritance of the saints in light, in His presence. Verse 12 tells me that I have been made fit for that day.

Here on earth, I am occasionally invited to a very "swell" banquet, but I always feel a little awkward. I hardly know what to do with all that hardware on the table; and all those gaudy waiters around, looking at me with their superior know-how, make me nervous. However, I have found out that my fellow guests are not much happier than I, and that makes me feel better.

Once, coming over from Europe on the Holland-America Line, we had fried chicken for dinner. Everyone very politely was trying to carve the chicken (which I think must have died from old age) with their knives, when the chicken leg on the plate of the gentleman next to me took a three-cornered jump across the table and landed in the lap of a bejewelled young lady across from me. She bawled him out in the French language in a rather unladylike way. Fortunately for him, he did not understand; but I did, and it revised my opinion of her as a lady, in consequence.

Well, to be on the safe side, I picked up my piece of chicken by both ends, and went at my dinner in a more satisfactory fashion. Looking down the long table a few moments later, I saw that every one of the diners had followed my example. I never knew until then what an influential character I really was. Well, praise God, in heaven I'll not only have eternal life, but I will know how to live it to perfection.

The Spirit convicted me and pointed me to Christ.
The Son is now my King, whom I seek to serve and obey.

The Father has made me fit for the Glory; thanks to His name.

Paul gives thanks for three things, as we have seen; three things that have been done for me, for (1) I have redemption; (2) I have been brought out of Satan's kingdom into the kingdom of Christ; and (3) I have been made meet for heaven. In view of these things which are so, Paul prays for three things that they might be so. He prays that I might be filled with His will; that I might walk worthy; and that I might increase in the knowledge of God. Or, in other words, that I might KNOW, and GO, and GROW.

# Reconciliation

*"And, having made peace through the blood of His cross, by Him to reconcile all things unto Himself; by Him, I say, whether they be things in earth, or things in heaven. And you, that were sometime alienated and enemies in your mind by wicked works, yet now hath He reconciled in the body of His flesh through death, to present you holy and unblameable and unreproveable in His sight."*

(Col. 1:20-22)

The Cross! That is where man poured out his gall, and where God poured forth His grace. Man was the offender, but the overture of forgiveness and reconciliation was ushered in .by God. He is going to reconcile all things, including man, unto Himself, whether in heaven or in earth.

Notice this! Some will tell you this means that every sinner, some day, shall be reconciled to God, but our text does not suggest that. There are three prominent spheres in

Scripture: heaven, earth and hell.

In our text, where reconciliation is the subject, only heaven and earth are given, for sinners in hell will never be reconciled to God. But in Philippians 2:10, where subjection is the thought, we read that every knee shall bow, even of those in hell. Every soul shall be subject to Christ, but only those who believe shall be reconciled.

God holds out the hand of reconciliation to His enemies, and those who accept His proffered grace are reconciled to Him, even though once enemies, by wicked works.

The story is told of a certain servant of Christ who walked about 100 miles (no small undertaking in those early days) to plead with President Washington for the life of a man who had been condemned to death. The President sadly said he was sorry, but he did not think that the circumstances warranted his interference, and told the preacher, "I'd like to do this for your friend, but feel that I shouldn't." "But," said the pleader, "he isn't my friend. He has been my bitter enemy for years. He has done all he could to slander and injure me and blacken my name; and I want to show him that I love him in spite of all." "In that case," replied Washington, with tears in his eyes, "how can I refuse? Your request is granted." And that is how, but so much more amazingly, our wonderful Lord seeks to bless His enemies.

We Christians have already been reconciled; the heavens and the earth are going to be. In a certain country, ages ago, an uprising against its ruler had been put down; and many of the rebels came to the king, bowing before him, seeking pardon. Some of the officers said: "Don't listen to them; they are rebels and deserve to die." But the sovereign, looking at the suppliants, said: "I see no rebels here." Neither does God when sinners bow humbly before Him, acknowledging their guilt. To such, He holds out the golden sceptre. What is the result of such gracious reconciliation? The result is that we are presented holy, blameless, and without reproof in His sight.

# Importance of Scripture

*"As ye have therefore received Christ Jesus the Lord, so walk ye in Him: rooted and built up in Him, and stablished in the faith, as ye have been taught, abounding therein with thanksgiving.*

*"Beware lest any man spoil you through philosophy and vain deceit, after the tradition of men, after the rudiments of the world, and not after Christ. For in Him dwelleth all the fulness of the Godhead bodily."*

(Col. 2:6-9)

There is great need for believers to be established in the faith, and this is not accomplished by having the head stuffed with a lot of knowledge of the Bible, but by the heart being enraptured with Christ. The believer is not only to receive the truth, but to receive Christ Jesus the Lord (verse 6); not merely to know the Scriptures, but to be built up in Him and rooted in Him; to walk in Him, for in Him all the fulness of God is pleased to dwell. The Scriptures ever point to Christ. They are like a signpost, and we are supposed to go whither that directs us.

The story is told of a man who sat on top of a road marker. When someone came along and asked him what he was doing there, he replied: "This sign says this goes to Burnham, and I'm waiting for it to start." Many believers act like that; they know and hug the Scripture verse, but they don't go to Him to whom the Word of God directs them.

In a certain wealthy home, the servant lifted the receiver when the telephone bell rang, and after listening for a moment said: "Yes, ma'am, sho' is," and hung up the receiver. This happened two more times till the lady of the house, overhearing this, said: "What are you saying, 'Yes, ma'am, sho' is' for?" She replied: "Why, madam, there's someone on the line say, 'Long distance from Washington', and it sho' is!" She agreed with the speaker, but she did not listen to the message.

Our text talks about going (walking), growing (rooted), and knowing (being built up), but all these must be in Him. He is to be our Life, our Food, our Light. In Him dwells all the fulness of the Godhead. Believers may know many things, but it is only knowing Him that will keep them from being led astray.

Paul says here: "Beware lest any man rob you of that which is of Christ." What they say may sound smart, but it is only empty philosophy, perhaps. Professors may think they know so much, but when it comes to divine truths, they are only in the elementary class, for they peddle the rudiments (the elements) of the world. Many a young Christian, going to a modern university, has had his faith shattered by the ramblings of some two-bit professor who knew no more about the Word of God than the fellow who said he'd like to believe the Bible, but he just couldn't swallow the impossible contention that the Israelites carried that big Noah's ark through the wilderness for forty years! Beware, says God, lest these philosophers rob you of everything true and real, and give you nothing in exchange.

I will never forget how a dear brother, with tears, told me how his son turned away from God's wondrous truth to take up with the empty, blatant vapourings of infidel writers. Speaking to his father, he said to him: "All you ever taught us is what the Bible says. Why didn't you tell us what others, from the other point of view, think and teach? Why did you only cram the Bible down our throats?"

His father gave him a truly splendid answer, I thought, when he said: "Why don't you bawl your mother out, too?" "Bawl my mother out? Why in the name of sense should I do that?"

His dad replied: "You should bawl her out for giving you bacon and eggs for breakfast, or pancakes and syrup; for not setting some garbage or sawdust before you some mornings. You want good food for your body, but you want swill for your soul. That's the reason we only taught you God's pure and holy Word."

But it is against such perversion that our text warns. It is not enough to be taught God's Word; the soul must practise the presence of God. It is not truth, but Christ who keeps and satisfies. All human speculation, all vain philosophy (that robs the soul of divine truth and gives nothing but hot air in exchange), is only of the most elementary character. The wiseacres of the world don't know it, but they actually are in the kindergarten, in the A-B-C class, while the believer in Jesus has entered upon the higher and highest branches of learning, for all true knowledge is resident in Christ - see verse 3 of this chapter.

He is the Alpha and the Omega - the first and the last letters of the Greek alphabet, and all the other letters in between. All language falls short to describe and encompass all He is and all the blessings flowing from Him to sinful man. Walk in Him, and your talk will make sense!

# Spiritual Constraints

*"Wherefore if ye be dead with Christ from the rudiments of the world, why, as though living in the world, are ye subject to ordinances, (Touch not; taste not; handle not; which all are to perish with the using;) after the commandments and doctrines of men?"*

(Col. 2:20-22)

A believer, since he has died with Christ, is, of course, no longer in the world, as far as God is concerned. I believe that's why it says in our text "as though living in the world". As to his bodily presence, he is in the world, but spiritually he lives in heaven.

He is not of this world, as Jesus says of him in John 17:16. Spiritually, his citizenship is in another world; it is in heaven, not upon the earth. He lives under a new form of government, no longer under law, but under grace. The law has executed him, as we read in Romans 7:11: "For sin, taking occasion by the commandment, deceived me, and by it slew me." Now the believer lives under the rule of grace (Rom. 6:14). Grace teaches him to live righteously, soberly and godly in this present world (Titus 2:12). He does not need the threat of punishment to keep him from doing wrong, nor the fear of God to stir him to do what's right.

A certain man claimed that all his neighbours were honest, and he need not worry about anyone stealing his chickens. Someone asked him, "If that is so, why do you keep that loaded shotgun always handy at the back door?" "That's to keep them honest," was the answer. But the real believer in Jesus does not need that. He has no desire whatever to steal; but he has a great desire to serve the Lord and to live for the blessing of his fellowmen; and to this, not fear, but the love of Christ constrains him.

Since the believer is free from the law, why go back to the elements of the world, when he has graduated into the highest university ever known - heaven's school of advanced superknowledge? He is not in the kindergarten, in the elementary class, where the chief lessons are of the negative variety - touch not, taste not, handle not. The "nots" are for infants in the elementary class, as we all know.

One of my sons was in a home some years ago, where a little boy of around four years or so took him all through the house and pointed out to him a number of things, saying: "This is a no-no, and that is a no-no." He knew all the no-no's in the house, but negatives don't produce anything. At the most, all they can accomplish is to restrain the manifestation of the sin that lurks within; but even that is largely a failure, for prohibitions do not reform; they only restrain.

A believer in Jesus is way above and beyond that type of rule. His life is a positive one of devotion to God and service to man. That is so only because, while the law only curbs the evil nature within (without, in any way at all, changing it), the grace of God has implanted in the soul the nature of

God Himself, pure and holy. This enables the believer to live a life of glad surrender, of deep love to Christ, and of positive blessing to those around in need of God's salvation.

# Believer's Sustenance

*"If ye then be risen with Christ, seek those things which are above, where Christ sitteth on the right hand of God. Set your affection on things above, not on things on the earth. For ye are dead, and your life is hid with Christ in God. When Christ, who is our life, shall appear, then shall ye also appear with Him in glory."*

(Col. 3:1-4)

Dead with Christ in chapter 2; risen with Christ in chapter 3. The antithesis to "dead" is "alive", but it does not use that word in our text, but, rather, "risen". That which rises comes from below, and the Spirit, as it were, would have us look down to the depth from which divine grace has brought us, that we may appreciate the more the heights to which that grace takes us.

Christ went down to the depths of woe in bearing our sins, and then He rose to the highest heights, and we, by faith, have died and risen with Him. Christ not only rose, but He ascended, and now sits above at the right hand of God. By faith, we are there, too, but actually we are still on earth. So, we are bidden to set our mind on things above, not on things on the earth. Again, our gaze is directed to Christ, as throughout this epistle.

Once, while I sat reading in our living room, my wife said to me: "August, what shall we have for dinner tonight?" I replied: "Yes, that'll be fine." "What did you say?" said she, and I could tell, by the puzzled tone of her voice, that I must have made some blunder. Said I: "What did you say?" Said she: "I asked you what we were to have for dinner tonight, and you said, 'Yes, that will be fine.'"

"Well, you see, my mind was somewhere else altogether. I heard some din or other, but did not really hear what you said." My body was in that chair, but I wasn't there. My mind was engaged right then with the things that are above, where Christ is.

The believer in Jesus, praise God, can have his body here on earth, but his heart and mind in the glory above. God desires this to be true of us whenever time or opportunity affords. Don't always be thinking of secular affairs. Take time to be holy - wholly occupied with Christ and spiritual realities.

"For ye are dead, and your life is hid with Christ in God" (Col. 3:3). The Christian is both dead and alive at the same time - dead to sin and alive to God. Both of these, of course, are in the spiritual realm, for we can't be both physically.

You may have heard of a man who lay extremely ill. Sad to say, his wife was not sorry to see him go. Bye and bye, the doctor, who was present at his bedside, could no longer feel a pulsebeat, and said to the wife: "He's gone." The patient opened his eyes and spoke up: "No, I ain't." Said his wife: "Hush up, John, the doctor knows more about those things than you do!" That's nonsense, of course, but spiritually it is exactly true. A believer seems dead when he yields to the flesh; he shows himself alive when he lives a godly life.

The life of the believer is hid with Christ in God. I don't think this means the life which the believer has, in this text, but, rather, the life he lives - his practical christian life and conduct. That life is hid, for Christ is the believer's life, as the next verse states, for it says that Christ is our life, and Christ is hid from human eyes. The believer alone sees Him, and that by faith.

Israel of old found nothing in the wilderness on which to subsist. Their food and drink had to be provided miraculously. Even so, there is nothing in this world to sustain the believer in Jesus. People sometimes wonder and say: "What do you Christians find to enjoy? What do you live on? What do you get out of life, anyway?"

The answer is that our life is in heaven. I like to use the illustration of the diver in this regard. There he is, down in the sea, perhaps a hundred feet or more beneath the surface, where it is impossible for man to live, yet he lives there. Perhaps the fishes, seeing him, ask each other: "What does that queer-looking monster live on? He does not have fins like we do; no gills with which to breathe; how does he manage to exist?"

We know the answer: the diver is in touch with the air above. He lives down below, but his life comes from above. He breathes the higher atmosphere. He gets his directions and supplies from above, too. When he needs something, he signals by way of the line he carries.

It is so exactly with the Christian. He lives because of contact with a risen and exalted Christ above; He is his life. Spiritual food, the water, bread, wine, oil, all come from heaven, through the ministry of the Spirit by the Word. There is absolutely nothing in this world for a child of God to feast or feed on.

But, some day, Christ shall come in power and glory, and then every eye shall see Him. People shall then recognize, when they see us coming with Him, dressed in dazzling beauty, that we weren't such fools, as the world often accounted us. Christ shall then be seen in all His glory, as He is to be seen today, in all His grace, in the lives of His saints.

# Peace of God

*"Let the peace of God rule in your hearts, to the which also ye are called in one body; and be ye thankful. Let the word of Christ dwell in you richly in all wisdom; teaching and admonishing one another in psalms and hymns and spiritual songs, singing with grace in your hearts to the Lord. And whatsoever ye do in word or deed, do all in the name of the Lord Jesus, giving thanks to God and the Father by Him."*

(Col. 3:15-17)

The peace of Christ is to be the "umpire" of our hearts, for that is the meaning of the word "rule". An umpire has a thankless job often because all parties want the verdict to be in their favour. But when Christ fills the heart, we want Him to have His way, and not us to have ours. Then the same peace which He knew, as He committed Himself completely to the Father's will, shall be ours, too, in full measure. It is that peace which He bequeathed unto us when He went back home, see John 14:27

The Word of Christ, when it has shone in us, will enrich our lives. We shall profit from help our fellowbelievers can give to us, and our hearts will be filled with praise to the Lord.

The latter part of verse 16 is a great comfort to many believers. They can't sing very sweetly with their voice, but can make heaven glad with the sweetness of melody coming from the heart, which exalts Christ.

This chapter starts out with the person of the Christ, verse 1; the forgiveness of Christ, verse 13; the peace of Christ, verse 15; the Word of Christ, verse 16; and the Lordship of Christ, also in verse 17. In this chapter, Christ is all and in all.

# Seasoned with Salt

*"Walk in wisdom toward them that are without, redeeming the time. Let your speech be alway with grace, seasoned with salt, that ye may know how ye ought to answer every man."*

(Col. 4:5-6)

Walk in verse 5, and talk in verse 6; neither is easy. It may be easy for some folks to talk, but a Christian should want to say something when he talks.

A black man went to a lawyer to see about a divorce. Said he: "I jes' can't take it any mo'; all dat woman does is talk, talk, and talk!" "What does she talk about so much?" asked the lawyer. Said the irritated husband: "She don' say."

In the days of King James, when the Authorized version of the Bible came into being, the word translated "conversation" then meant conduct or walk; but since that day, folks have done so much talking and so little walking that the word now means talk.

Believers are to walk in wisdom in their relation to the unsaved ones around, and are to buy up the opportunities of witnessing for their Lord. Towards believers, they are to speak with grace (grace is to be the main course), but it must be seasoned with salt.

Grace and truth came by Jesus Christ. We have these two in our verse. Sugar and salt; grace and truth. Grace is sweet; salt we use in lesser doses. Truth, as we all know, is not very popular, but it is very necessary. Nobody wants too much of it, so it has to be used just for seasoning.

A lady went to a photographer to have her portrait taken. The most charitable thing you could have said of her is that she never would have won a prize in a beauty contest. When she came to pick up her pictures, she stormed at the photographer: "They are terrible! I won't pay for them; they don't do me justice." "Ma'am," said the exasperated man, "with a face like yours, what you need is not justice, but mercy!" You see, she didn't relish the truth about herself; neither do you or I.

Many times physicians prescribe a no-salt diet. Salt in the system raises the blood pressure, they say. And, certainly not strange, the salt of our text does the same. The truth of God has a way of raising the soul's blood pressure often to a dangerous pitch.

It boiled over in the case of the Pharisees, when the truth our blessed Lord spoke and lived before them exploded in their rejection and crucifixion of Him. But believers can stand a little of it; yet, even there it calls for real skill to administer the right dose. It is best to slip it in under a thick coating of the sugar of grace.

A soft answer turns away wrath; and a proper dose of grace, seasoned with the salt of truth, not only will keep the blood pressure from causing a stroke, but will provide the right remedy required to save the sinner, to restore the fallen saint, and to encourage the weary child of God.

# Spirit, Soul, and Body

*"And the very God of peace sanctify you wholly; and I pray God your whole spirit and soul and body be preserved blameless unto the coming of our Lord Jesus Christ."*

(1 Thess. 5:23)

SPIRIT. Folks nearly always speak of body, soul and spirit, but God, as you see in this text, puts the spirit first and the body last.

Man, blinded by Satan, magnifies the physical; with God, the spiritual is of more importance. With his human spirit, man knows the things of man (1 Cor. 2:11); even so, with the Holy Spirit, only those saved and indwelt by Him can know the things of God (1 Cor. 2:12).

Through sin, man's spirit has become darkened and alienated from the life of God (Eph. 4:18); and his spirit needs to be renewed through the lifegiving power of the Holy Spirit, creating new birth. That's what we read in Romans 12:2; Ephesians 4:23; Titus 3:5, etc.

Through the impartation of divine life and the indwelling Spirit of God, all human faculties become more acute, for the mind is renewed (Rom. 12:2); the heart is enlarged (2 Cor. 6:11) and here is where an enlarged heart is nothing to be alarmed about; the eyes are enlightened (Eph. 1:18); and the ears are circumcised or opened (Acts 7:51). It is a complete job of spiritual rehabilitation. Now the believer is able to grasp, appreciate, and convey to others the truths which have to do with the knowledge of God and fellowship with God.

With the spirit, we know. It is the seat of understanding. The Christian knows, first of all, because God says so; secondly, because he lives out the truths wrought within him by the Spirit.

There is a beautiful picture of this in the woman who had

the issue of blood, as recorded in Mark 5. Through a touch of faith, she was instantly healed. Probably bashful with so many folks around, she was about to withdraw unnoticed, without anyone knowing the miracle that had taken place; but Jesus would not let her. He knew she had been healed, but He wanted others to know, too. When she found she could not be hidden, she came and fell down before Him; and, in the presence of that vast concourse, she told the story of her desperate need and of His saving power.

Then the Lord said to her: "Daughter, thy faith hath made thee whole; go in peace and be whole of thy plague." Now, why did Jesus say to her "be whole of thy plague" when she already was whole? Was it not to confirm the miracle and assure her that the cure was a permanent one? Suppose she had gotten away without confessing Him as her Saviour?

Perhaps, the next day or two, not feeling well one morning, she might have said to herself: "Perhaps I was not healed after all; it probably was just the excitement of the moment; I feel as if the trouble is still with me." But now she could never think that any more. She not only had the healing her faith had secured for her, but she had His word for it that it was sure.

So, we get saved by faith, but we get assurance by confessing Him. We get to know Him and His Word experimentally. What a vast realm of knowledge lies open before the child of God! What an incentive to study, digest, enjoy and share the wonderful things of God! By the power of God's Spirit, our human spirit can grasp the infinite wonders of divine truth.

SOUL. The soul is the seat of the affections and passions. It is, in Scripture, almost a synonym for the most wonderful passion of all - the ability to love.

In the human realm, it has been said that love is the perfect tense of the verb "live". "The greatest of these is love" (1 Cor. 13:13).

In the Old Testament, the command was, "Thou shalt love the Lord thy God with all thy heart," etc. (Luke 10:27). Man could not do this, and God knew this. Now we listen to the very reverse, "The Lord thy God loves thee", for "God so loved the world that He gave His only begotten Son." God not only told us this, but He proved it.

Man glibly talks of love, but it is often like that of the young swain who wrote his beloved that he loved her enough to go through fire, water and blood for her. Then, at the foot of his letter, he added: "P. S. If it does not rain tonight, I am coming to see you." But God wrote His love in fire and blood on the Cross of Calvary.

The Greeks magnified intellect; the Romans worshipped power; but Christianity has introduced the glorious concept of love as the mightiest power in the universe. Love is synonymous with sacrifice; love gives. Even in minor details, it ever gives. How well this is seen in a mother with her family; she is always sacrificing, yet seems little aware of it.

There are many verses in the New Testament bidding a believer to show love to others, but not one that I know of where we are told to look for it.

I remember so well that, years ago, a certain young brother left the assembly he was in because, he said, some brother had not shown him christian love. So, I went to see him for a little talk; and when he brought this up, I told him that he was wrong in his attitude.

Said I: "When I proposed to the lady who is now my wife, I did not say to her, 'Miss Roberts, don't you think you ought to love me? I'm a good looking fellow, healthy and strong; I've got a good job - I'm a preacher, and I'll never be out of work (I couldn't say much for the pay, and I still can't). Don't you think you ought to love me?' If I had talked to her that way, she would rightly have considered me to be a little touched in the head. You don't ask a girl to love you; you tell her that you love her, and then you try to show it a little, too."

Once the love of God has found a response in your heart, or rather has created it there, then you love Him in return. Your love to Him can only be shown in your love towards others, specially towards believers, for again and again we are urged to love one another. This is not always easy, as suggested in this cute little verse:

To dwell above with the saints we love,
Oh, that will be grace and glory;
But to dwell below with the saints we know,
Ah, that's a different story!

A wife, rebuking her husband for his lack of kindness to her, reminded him that, before their marriage, he had told her he loved her so much that he could die for her. "Yes, I know," he replied, "but I have found out it would be easier to die for you than to live with you!" That's a little strong, naturally, but the general principle is true: living daily a life of devotion and responsive love to Christ requires all the power of God.

BODY. The only part of us that those around us actually see is our body. In our relation to others, it is the most important, while, toward God, our spirit and soul take the precedence. My body is not only the link between the world and me, but between the world and Christ, for Christ liveth in me. He dwells within my body, and He is to be magnified in my body.

What an importance this gives to the body of the believer! The natural man has a perverted sense of the proper use of the body. It is not to be used for a clothes rack; it is not a furnace to be stoked with food; it is not a face to be painted, nor a bunch of sinews and muscles to be trained for physical prowess.

Its proper function is to display Christ to a world in sin, and the believer must keep that in mind. As the body without the human spirit is dead, so the body without the Holy Spirit is spiritually dead. But, by the indwelling of the Spirit, it becomes, as it were, spiritually alive and can be presented to God as a living sacrifice, holy, acceptable to Him (Rom. 12:1).

Present, or yield, your body, says Romans 12:1. Yielding suggests weakness. For successful Christian living, I am to furnish the weakness and God will furnish the strength; I furnish the body, and He supplies the Spirit. "Ye are not your own; therefore glorify God in your body, which is His." (1 Cor. 6:19-20).

We are to be blameless unto the coming of our Lord Jesus Christ. Spirit, soul and body are to be preserved blameless till that day. We are to live our life always in view of that day when the Lord comes to take us home, and when our path shall be reviewed and we shall be rewarded at the Judgment Seat of Christ.

# Conscience

*"Now the end of the commandment is charity (love) out of a pure heart, and of a good conscience, and of faith unfeigned."*

(1 Timothy 1:5)

We must ascertain which commandment is "the" commandment of our text. "The" is a very exclusive word and limits it to one. However, I can right now think of another occasion where we read of one commandment.

When the Mosaic law was given, there were vastly more commandments than one, but long before that, in the Garden of Eden, God gave Adam and Eve just one commandment: they were forbidden to eat of the tree of the knowledge of good and evil.

However, that cannot be the commandment of our text, for the end of that (the result of keeping it) is said to be a good conscience, and we all know that the result of the one commandment in Eden was the exact reverse. That one commandment produced, in our first parents, not a good, but an evil, accusing conscience.

Conscience was born in paradise, and it had a very nasty start. The devil was the salesman who sold it to our first parents: "Eat of that tree," said he, "and you'll be like God, knowing good and evil." They did, and conscience came into existence. They learned to know, by themselves, without God; and they learned to know too much.

That's what the word "conscience" means. It means a knowing within; a knowledge which was gained through disobedience to God. They got an ability to know good and evil, without the power to do the good or to refrain from doing the evil. Quite a science - that conscience! Our scientists ought to study that science a little more.

But they can't do it, really, because their consciences (and the consciences of all sinners) are twisted, perverted and often totally incapacitated to do proper research work. The Bible says that man's conscience is defiled; that it needs cleansing, that it is evil and, through habitual failure to heed it, it becomes seared as with a hot iron, and does not work anymore at all.

No, the commandment given to Adam can't be the one of our text, for that produced an evil conscience. It requires a more excellent commandment to furnish the good conscience of our text.

I believe it is the commandment of 1 John 3:23: "And this is His commandment, That we should believe on the name of His Son Jesus Christ, and love one another, as He gave us commandment." Love, the wondrous love of Christ towards us, produces in the heart of the believer the responsive love that flows from a pure heart and a good conscience; for, when the sinner receives the great love of God in his heart, his conscience is renovated by that love.

We read in Hebrews 10:22, "having our hearts sprinkled from an evil conscience, and our bodies washed with pure water"; or, as we read again in Hebrews 9:14, "How much more shall the blood of Christ...purge your conscience from dead works to serve the living God." With a new life in Christ comes a new conscience - now all fixed, adjusted and oiled to run properly.

In the days when we had babies in the family, sometimes one of them would cry in the night, but I did not hear it. When my wife would gently chide me once in a while, I'd say: "Well, you see, I sleep so soundly because I have a good conscience." But she'd come back with: "You sleep and let me get up with the baby because you have no conscience!" But she was wrong. I had a conscience alright; a good one, brand new because I used it so little, at least in that connection. But the believer has a good conscience, and he is to use it for the glory of God.

Five times in the New Testament we believers are said to have a "good" conscience. But we need to see to it that we listen to its voice, and this will be so when love out of a pure heart operates. Sometimes Christians, when approached in regard to some weakness or sin in their lives, will say: "I don't have any conscience about this", when actually they should have. What is their trouble?

The root cause is that they are lacking in love to Christ, lacking in appreciation of the love of Christ to them, even as was the case with me when I let my wife get up at nights with our babies. Had I loved her in a practical way, as I should have, I would have insisted on getting up. (I don't want you to think I was always that callous.)

The love of God in the heart results in a pure heart, a good conscience and unfeigned faith. Notice that the heart comes first; then the conscience. Out of the heart are the issues of life. If love is real, then life will be realistic.

A mother told her boy, when he came home from school, to hang out the living room rug and beat it. Much later that day, when he came in from playing ball, his mother asked: "Didn't I tell you to take the rug out and beat it?" "So I did, Mother," said he, "I hung the rug on the line, and then I beat it, just as you told me!" (Only he "beat it" for the ball field.)

You see, if he had loved his mother the way he should have, instead of loving himself and his own desires, he would not have abused her command, though the words permitted the interpretation he put on them. Now, if he had listened to his conscience at all, it would have had an accusing tone; it was bad instead of good.

As Paul said of himself, may we all crave always "to have a good conscience, void of offence toward God and toward men" (Acts 24:16).

# Joy of the Lord

*"According to the glorious gospel of the blessed God, which was committed to my trust."*

(1 Timothy 1:11)

A more accurate rendering here would be "the glorious gospel of the happy God". I like that! The glory of the happy God is to make others happy. There is a proverb that says that misery loves company, but that is totally untrue. It is happiness that loves company; when you are happy, you always want to share this with others. It has been well said that sorrow, shared with others, cuts it in half; while joy, shared with others, doubles it.

God is a happy God, and it is His glory to make others happy. God found His joy in the society of His beloved Son. In Proverbs 8:30 we hear our Saviour say: "I was by Him, as one brought up with Him: and I was daily His delight, rejoicing always before Him." God found His joy in Christ from all eternity, and He said, as it were: "I am so happy knowing and having My beloved Son; I'll send Him to earth so that the sons of men may come to know Him and be happy, too." And so the announcement was made in due time: "I bring you good tidings of great joy, which shall be to all people. For unto you is born this day in the city of David a Saviour, which is Christ the Lord" (Luke 2:10-11).

Our Lord was very happy down here, though at the same time He was the Man of sorrows and acquainted with grief. He could say: "I delight to do the Father's will." He did not merely do God's will because it had to be done, but He delighted in doing it, even though it meant the Cross with its fearful suffering. He prayed for His disciples that His joy might be fulfilled in them (John 17:13).

On one occasion, a very solemn-looking speaker addressed a class of children and, among other things, said:

"The Lord Jesus never smiled or laughed." A little girl spoke up and said: "I believe He did!" "Why, my dear?" said he. "Because," answered the little miss, "if He had looked as sad as you do, little children never would have come to Him!" I believe there is a good deal of truth in that.

In the same connection, I remember a very lovable servant of Christ telling of a time when he was riding on a streetcar in Capetown, South Africa. At one stop, a lady got on with a little girl of around five or six. The lady sat down on the last empty seat available and whispered something in the child's ear. Upon this, the child looked all through the car and finally, way back at the other end of the car, sat down on the lap of the dear old Christian.

Relating this, he told me: "My, how thrilled I was. 'Just think of it,' I said to myself, 'this dear little girl picked me out from all these folks as the one she could trust. Apparently I must really look good and kind to her.' And then, suddenly, I checked myself," said he. "'Why, you old sinner, you are lifted up with pride and admiring yourself. You are only a disciple, and don't you remember that the disciples turned away the children when they came to Jesus?'" And then the thought struck him, "If I, as a disciple (and they drive children away), could draw this little one to me, then how attractive the Lord Jesus must have been!"

God is indeed the happy God, and happiness is contagious. He came down to bring heaven's joy to us. In that wonderful 15th chapter of Luke, in each of the three stories told, the emphasis is on the joy that fills heaven and earth when a soul turns to God, and this is reflected in the joy of the soul thus saved by grace.

# Office v. Work

*"This is a true saying, If a man desire the office of a bishop, he desireth a good work.*

*"Likewise must the deacons be grave, not doubletongued, not given to much wine, not greedy of filthy lucre; holding the mystery of the faith in a pure conscience. And let these also first be proved; then let them use the office of a deacon, being found blameless.*

*"For they that have used the office of a deacon well purchase to themselves a good degree, and great boldness in the faith which is in Christ Jesus."*

(1 Timothy 3:1, 8-10, 13)

So that you know, the translators of the King James version were enamoured of officialism. Actually, that word "office", found three times in this chapter, does not exist at all in the Greek language.

There are still lots of folks, even true Christians at times, who love to have an office. Many employers complain that lots of men are looking for a job, but few are looking for work. There are not so many real deacons around (the word means something like "raising dust by being in a hurry").

Have you heard the story of a certain fellow who got fired by his boss? A customer, entering the country store, said to the proprietor: "Where's Elmer?" "Elmer ain't here," was the laconic answer. "Do you mean that Elmer is out somewhere on an errand?" "Nope, he just ain't here no more." "You mean he quit?" "Nope." "Are you telling me you fired him?" "Yep." "Did you get anybody to fill the vacancy?" The taciturn storekeeper replied: "Elmer didn't leave no vacancy!"

God wants workers; not shirkers. God delights in those who want to live for Christ, and to serve Him and His people because they delight to do so, without expecting remuneration or recognition by man. Not like the brother who often prayed: "Lord, make me a doormat for my brethren." Then, when someone stepped on him pretty hard one day, he resented it quite vociferously. Another brother said dryly: "This is the first time in my life I have ever heard a doormat squeal."

Lowly service is not popular, nor is it easy. It calls for real grace and patience. But it is the steppingstone towards greater usefulness and greater spiritual power, for we read in verse 13 that those who serve well as deacons purchase to themselves a good degree and great boldness in the faith.

It is necessary to start at the bottom in the menial tasks for which one is fitted, and then to advance in capacity as one grows in grace and spiritual ability. Don't be like the little wrist watch that said, while looking up at Big Ben in London: "My, I wish I was up there, so that all of London could look at me." All of a sudden, so the fantasy goes, the little watch felt itself whisked upward, way, way up, till it found itself on the gigantic dial of Big Ben. It got its wish but, alas, nobody could see it now, for its elevation had become its annihilation.

According to verse 13, God sells college degrees. However, they are not secured by education, but by perspiration; not by brain, but by brawn. They are not sold for money, as honorary degrees are sometimes sold, but are bought with humble, diligent service in the work of the Lord. Such degrees God will honour at the graduation exercises in heaven, when He confesses His servants before His Father - when earthly honours will have crumbled into dust.

# God-likeness

*"And without controversy great is the mystery of godliness: God was manifest in the flesh, justified in the Spirit, seen of angels, preached unto the Gentiles, believed on in the world, received up into glory."*

(1 Timothy 3:16)

Do you want to be like God? Here is the secret as to how to attain that great goal. Here is the secret of godliness - Godlikeness.

In the Garden of Eden, man lost his likeness to God, for we read that after sin came, Adam begat a son in his likeness (Gen. 5:3); not in God's likeness. The tempter beguiled our parents by suggesting that, through disobedience, they would become like God, knowing good and evil. They did become like God in a certain sense, but alas, without the capacity to do good or to withstand evil. They lost their likeness to God and became, as did all their descendants, ungodly.

But then, praise His name, God became manifest in flesh when Christ was born. He came in the likeness of sinful flesh, but only in the likeness of it, for He Himself was and is pure and holy, sinless. He became like us and, as a man, took all our sins and guilt upon Himself, in order that He might make us like Him. Man, saved by grace, will some day be completely like God, for when we see Him, we shall be like Him, for we shall see Him as He is. We shall be like Him - not by our climbing up, but by God's coming down to us in all our sin and shame. Blessed be His Name!

Christ was justified in spirit. His whole life, in every detail, proved Him to be sinless and holy. His life was His credentials, proving He had indeed the fitness and the power to be the Saviour of sinners.

He was seen of angels. They watched with adoring wonder when He came to earth as a Babe in Bethlehem;

when He trod His earthly path; when He prayed in Gethsemane; when He died on Calvary; and when He rose again upon the first day of the week. Too bad that men are so indifferent to "the things the angels desire to look into" (1 Peter 1:12).

Now the last three statements of our text carry us beyond the death and ascension of Christ on to this present day of grace, and thus take in, in their scope, the saints of God. For Christ was not preached unto the Gentiles during His life on earth, nor believed on in the world. That is true today, since the Cross. So, I take it, the final statement, "received up into glory", has in view Christ's entering into heaven when He brings us with Him at the rapture of the Church. We shall be received up into glory with Him. Then we shall truly be like Him in every way, changed into His likeness of glory, in body as well as soul and spirit (Phil. 3:20-21).

God wants us to become more like Him each day morally, which will be so when we gaze upon Him by faith (2 Cor. 3:18). He wants our hearts to be enraptured with Him.

Not like the little black boy who was met on the street one day by a lady. Said she: "And what's your name, sonny?" "Mah name is George Washington."

"Oh, that is a great name and so nice; I hope you try to live like him." "Like who?" "Why, like George Washington, of course." "Well," said the boy, "Ah can't help livin' like George Washington. Ah *is* George Washington!" He did not know any Washington greater than himself.

But we do know Him who is God over all, blessed forever, and we should crave to be like Him.

# Food and Exercise

*"If thou put the brethren in remembrance of these things, thou shalt be a good minister of Jesus Christ, nourished up in the words of faith and of good doctrine, whereunto thou hast attained. But refuse profane and old wives' fables, and exercise thyself rather unto godliness.*

*"For bodily exercise profiteth little: but godliness is profitable unto all things, having promise of the life that now is, and of that which is to come."*

(1 Timothy 4:6-8)

These are truly sensible words of great practical value to the believer in Jesus. They speak of the need of food and exercise, both of which are so important to spiritual health and growth.

The sixth verse seems to suggest that, by ministering the Word of God to others, the minister (servant) himself is fed, nourished up in faith and good teaching. The best way to grow is to feed others, for that forces you to go to the Word for light and instruction. There is need for sound doctrine, which is the technical way of saying that the believer needs solid food.

The athlete training for physical feats does not feed on fancy pastries, as Christians sometimes go for happy and peppy talks and similar superficial stuff. On such a diet, the believer will be half starved. You can't grow strong on a doughnut and a cup of coffee; you need a large juicy steak, which you have to chew and digest, and which stays with you.

Don't feed on profane and old wives' fables. That word "profane" has an interesting meaning; it is a combination of "threshhold" and "stepping" across it, thus suggesting, as it were, an open door for anyone to step in or out. It may suggest the wide open broadmindedness which is so popular in corrupt Protestantism (believe what you like);

while, in the fables of old wives, we can see the foolish, fanciful myths which Catholicism has its votaries swallow.

The true believer will not be fooled either way, but will take some strenuous exercise in the development of spiritual strength and growth in the knowledge of God's wonderful Word, and in corresponding Godlikeness. Godliness is profitable unto all things, not only for the present life, but for the life to come. A man that is formed, reformed, informed, and transformed by exercise in the precious things of Christ is better equipped than anyone else.

"The life that now is" and "that which is to come": live the present life for Him, and we'll enjoy the life to come with Him.


# Example to Others


*"Let no man despise thy youth; but be thou an example of the believers, in word, in conversation, in charity, in spirit, in faith, in purity. Till I come, give attendance to reading, to exhortation, to doctrine.*

*"Neglect not the gift that is in thee, which was given thee by prophecy, with the laying on of the hands of the presbytery.*

*"Meditate upon these things; give thyself wholly to them; that thy profiting may appear to all. Take heed unto thyself, and unto the doctrine; continue in them: for in doing this thou shalt both save thyself, and them that hear thee."*

(1 Timothy 4:12-16)

Timothy was not to neglect "himself". Seven times Paul urges him to think of "thyself":

Behave thyself in the house of God - 1 Tim. 3:15.

Exercise thyself unto godliness - 1 Tim. 4:7.

Give thyself wholly to these things - 1 Tim. 4:15.

Take heed to thyself - 1 Tim. 4:16.

Save thyself and them that hear thee - 1 Tim. 4:16.

Keep thyself pure - 1 Tim. 5:22.

Show thyself approved unto God - 2 Tim. 2:15.

Timothy was to be an example in word, conduct, love, faith, purity; in other words, he was to be an example to all believers in what he said, did, felt, believed and lived. He was to make sure his own life was right ere he ministered to others. He was to read, exhort, teach, and not to neglect the gift divinely bestowed upon him of imparting God's truth to others.

He was to go further than just reading; he was to meditate upon, and give himself wholly to, these precious spiritual things. Sometimes we are apt to read or hear the Word, and that's all.

We should be like the person who asked for a ham sandwich at a drive-in. "Do you want to eat it here or take it along?" asked the attendant. "Both!" was the answer. Do you do that? Or do you do with the Bible, as you do with the traffic light: stop when it is red (read)?

First, we should digest the Word and then apply it to others as the fruit of personal experience. There are some other Christians who hardly get anything at all when the Word is ministered to them.

A well known servant of Christ said at one time that some folks don't have as much sense as a chicken; for a chicken will pick over a whole bushel of chaff to find a few grains of wheat, while Christians will pick to pieces a bushel of wheat to find one speck of "chaff". The only thing they take away from the service is something the speaker did or said which they didn't like, or with which they didn't agree.

A man was invited to a very elegant dinner and, when asked later how he had enjoyed the meal, he completely omitted any mention whatever of all the wonderful food that was served and replied, "I don't like tomato soup!"

Meditate, Timothy was told. Chew the cud, beat out the grain, as Ruth did. She did not carry that big, unwieldy bundle of straw home, but beat out the chaff and kept the real food to enjoy. And don't stumble over things you don't understand, either; just enjoy what you do glean from the Word.

The tale is told of two men who were dining together, one a pronounced unbeliever. "How do you explain this and that and that in the Bible?" he asked. "Well, you see," said the other, "I do with the study of the Scriptures as I do with this fish we are eating. I just enjoy the fish, and when I come to a bone, I lay it to one side." "Yes, that is fine," said the other, "but what about the bones?" "Oh, I just let an infidel like you chew on the bones!"

# Earthly Possessions

*"Godliness with contentment is great gain. For we brought nothing into this world, and it is certain we can carry nothing out. And having food and raiment let us be therewith content.*

*"But they that will be rich fall into temptation and a snare, and into many foolish and hurtful lusts, which drown men in destruction and perdition. For the love of money is the root of all evil: which while some coveted after, they have erred from the faith, and pierced themselves through with many sorrows."*

(1 Timothy 6:6-10)

Here is the money-grubber's portrait; it presents a picture none of us ought ever to forget.

The first is that you can't take it with you. We brought nothing into this world, and we can carry nothing out. But, praise God, the believer, while he too, can't take things with him, he can send them on ahead. He can and should lay up treasures in heaven.

A worldly rich man would like to do two things when he dies - leave his sins here, and take his money with him; but he has to do the very reverse. However, the child of God does leave his sins, and all that is of sin, behind when he goes home to glory; and he can send his money on before by spending it now for the glory of God and the blessing of souls. The love of money is the root of nothing but evil - not money, but the love of it.

I said once to a dear old Christian: "It would be a wonderful thing to have a million dollars, wouldn't it?" "Yes, indeed," said he, "but a terrible thing to hanker after."

A love of money in the sinner leads to destruction and perdition, as witness the rich man of Luke 12, or the rich man of Luke 16 who opened his eyes in hell. In the Christian, it may lead to erring from the faith and a string of trouble and sorrow.

Money itself never made anybody happy, least of all the believer in Jesus; but it can be used to bring true joy to others. One of the most foolish quirks of human nature is to have money and not to use it.

One time a tenant of a rich English lord asked him if he would permit him to get a glimpse of his wealth. After some pleading, the nobleman (in name at least) showed him his vault, with its vast stores of money and securities, after which the farmer said: "Thank you very much, my lord; now I am just as rich as you are." "How do you arrive at that conclusion?" "Why," came the reply, "all you do is look at it; you never spend any of it; and now that I have looked at it too, I am just as rich as you."

Men strive after earthly possessions, which they have to leave when they leave here. That is sad enough, but it is even sadder that no mere things can bring them real joy or satisfaction even here and now.

An elderly couple lived near a railroad track; and one day, as they were rocking on their front porch, the husband said: "I wonder what that dog of ours is always chasing those trains for?" "That's not what bothers me," said the wife. "What I wonder about is what he is going to do with it if he ever catches one!" Sure enough, what? And what do people do with their money but worry about it, or get it stolen from them, etc.?

The story is told of a British millionaire named Sir Titus Saul, who had amassed a fortune and was now retired, in the sunset years of his life. One day, as he walked in his beautiful garden, he noticed a snail slowly and laboriously climbing up a bare stick which had once supported a rose bush. The snail was looking for a nice, fresh green leaf to eat. When it finally reached the top, it felt around for a few minutes and then, disappointed in finding nothing there, turned around and slowly started to crawl down.

"That's me," said the tycoon to himself. "I have found my way to the top from the bottom of society. Once I was a poor and illiterate boy, but by perseverance and application, I have reached the zenith; but there is nothing there. I am like that snail; disappointed and heartsick, I too am on the way down - down to where?"

It pays, doesn't it, to lay up there in the glory? The rich man in Luke 12 said to himself: "Soul, thou hast much goods laid up for many years; take thine ease, eat, drink, and be merry", but it was not so, for he died that night. Paul, in happy contrast, could say: "Henceforth there is laid up for me a crown of righteousness which the Lord, the righteous Judge, shall give to me in that day, and not to me only, but to all them also that love His appearing."

# Fleeing; Following; Fighting

*"But thou, O man of God, flee these things; and follow after righteousness, godliness, faith, love, patience, meekness. Fight the good fight of faith, lay hold on eternal life, whereunto thou art also called, and hast professed a good profession before many witnesses."*

(1 Timothy 6:11-12)

Timothy, and every Christian, should be a "4-F" soldier of the Lord. In the last world war, to be 4-F meant you were rejected for active military duty; but in God's army, you must be in that category to be of use. Even 5-B's are most acceptable in the army of the Lord, for in this war it is not physical prowess that counts, but spiritual strength and stamina.

Those rated 5-B's are said to be those who have the bald heads, bi-focals, bridges, bulges and bunions. Even if afflicted with all these five, you are still welcome in His service. Perhaps you are more useful, rather than less, for in this war, age fits the saint who has learned much in the school of hard knocks. Veterans are very much appreciated in this fight of faith.

Whether sinner or saint, one has to start by being a coward. The first command to be obeyed is to "flee"; then come following, fighting and faith. Those are the four F's.

A sinner should acknowledge his utter inability to face the wrath of God upon him, and is told to flee from the wrath to come. When God tells a soul to flee from, He also provides a place to flee to. Instead of fleeing from God, the sinner should flee to God, as David says in Psalm 143:9: "I flee unto Thee to hide me;" or again in Psalm 32:7: "Thou art my hiding place."

It is a wise thing to admit one's total helplessness in the matter of one's soul's salvation and to turn to God for refuge from the storm to come. God is close to the sinner;

the Bible says that He is not far from every one of us (Acts 17:27).

A traveller asked someone how far it was to the next town, which he named. "Oh," said the other, "I should say, roughly speaking, about 25,000 miles." "You are joking," said the inquirer. "No, indeed, I am not. The way you are headed now, you've got to go all the way around the earth to get to it; but just turn around, and you'll be there in ten minutes."

Even so, the sinner is a long way from God, as far as heaven is from hell, with his back turned towards God. But turn around, in other words, repent, for that's the idea of a turnabout face, and you'll be in His presence. He is near, ever ready to save anyone who comes to Him.

Then, after having been saved by the grace of God, the believer, too, needs to flee often. The Christian has three great opposing forces against him - the world, the flesh and the devil. He is told to flee from the first two, but never to flee from Satan. In verse 11 of our text, he is advised to flee "these things", and those things are the ones the worldling is so occupied with.

Singled out from them is the love of money, the root of only evil. Next, the believer is told to flee youthful lusts (2 Tim. 2:22).

You may have heard that, one day, St. Augustine met one of his former female companions on the street. When he saw her, he started running down the street, as she stopped to have a talk with him. "Why do you run, Augustine?" said she. "It is only I." "Ah," said the recent believer in Jesus, "but I run because it is not I." He felt he could not trust in his own strength, so he ran away. The believer is told to do so too, and to run to God - to flee to the refuge, to the Christ who sits at God's right hand as our High Priest, to provide grace and help in every time of need (Heb. 4:16).

We are to flee, and next we are to follow, not by ourselves, but "with them that call on the Lord out of a pure heart" (2 Tim. 2:22). We need the support, comfort and strength imparted by fellowship with other saints. We are not to go through the christian life as "lone rangers".

We must fight the good fight of faith. We have no armour for the back, as Ephesians 6 shows. We must always resist the devil, and then he will flee from us. If you turn your back to the world and to self, you will be spiritually qualified to fight the fight of faith; that is, to seek to win souls to Christ; to turn them from darkness to light, and from the power of Satan unto God; and also to contend earnestly for the faith once delivered to the saints.

So, we shall lay hold on eternal life; or, as it actually reads here, to lay hold on life that is truly life.

# Mothers

*"Greatly desiring to see thee, being mindful of thy tears, that I may be filled with joy; When I call to remembrance the unfeigned faith that is in thee, which dwelt first in thy grandmother Lois, and thy mother Eunice; and I am persuaded that in thee also."*

(2 Timothy 1:4-5)

It is truly a wonderful blessing to have had an upbringing in a christian home. What a vocation is that of a christian mother! How much, how very much, thousands and ten thousands of prominent believers in Jesus owe to their mothers! If all mothers were only believers, and concerned with the training of their children in the nurture and admonition of the Lord, there would be no need for public preaching of the gospel, for all would be saved as a result of home influence.

My own dear mother, whom I have never appreciated as I should have, brought up all her twelve children in His ways, so that eventually every one of them came to trust

Christ as Saviour; and some of them have spent their lives in seeking to minister Christ to others. Alas, all mothers are not Christians, any more than all mothers are good cooks.

A customer in a restaurant asked whether they had any pie for dessert. "Do we? I should say so!" was the answer. "The kind Mother used to make!" "Give me some ice cream, then," was the answer. Apparently the customer did not have any happy memories of his mother's baking ability.

Today, there are too many cigarette-smoking mothers and the gallivanting kind that seldom is at home. When our youngest son was in his teens, he often brought friends home with him after school. Several times he was told: "Boy, I wish I had a mother like yours; she is always here when you get home from school; but my mother is always out somewhere."

There used to be a time when every baby sitter had the same name, and that name was "Mother". It used to be said that "the hand that rocks the cradle is the hand that rules the world". But no hand rocks the cradle now in millions of homes, and, as a result, the devil rocks the world. Even christian mothers ought to be more awake, in many cases, to their responsibilities to their children and to their God, and that goes for fathers, too.

It is a most rewarding task, as Moses' mother found out when she committed her son in faith to God. Eventually, she heard those cheering words: "Take this child away and nurse it for me, and I will give thee thy wages" (Exodus 2:9). She got paid for bringing up her own child, and so will every christian mother.

That pay will exist in the love and response of her children to her; in their conversion early or later to God; and in the reward she will receive at the Judgment Seat of Christ.

# Death and Life

*"Be not thou therefore ashamed of the testimony of our Lord, nor of me His prisoner: but be thou partaker of the afflictions of the gospel according to the power of God; who hath saved us, and called us with an holy calling, not according to our works, but according to His own purpose and grace, which was given us in Christ Jesus before the world began,*

*"But is now made manifest by the appearing of our Saviour Jesus Christ, who hath abolished death, and hath brought life and immortality to light through the gospel."*

(2 Timothy 1:8-10)

The christian life is not all sweetness and light. Many are willing enough to partake of the blessings of the gospel, who are not so ready to partake of its afflictions. It costs something to be true to Christ; to bear testimony to Him, who is still rejected and by the few enthroned.

Paul says that the power of God is needed for this, and God has given us, not the spirit of fear, but of power, of love and of a sound mind. Not power alone, but power balanced by love, controlled by spiritual common sense. Power without love becomes ruthless; love without a sound mind degenerates into weakness. Power and love in Him combine, and are available to us.

Verse 10 speaks of "death" and "life" - two great mysteries. We usually put life first and then death; but through divine grace, that order has been reversed for the believer, and for him it is now death and life, in that order.

For the natural man, death is the king of terrors, as Job calls it (Job 18:14). It is the terror of kings, as well. Death always wins the battle in the end, except in the case of One, of whom our text speaks.

A brother in England, whose father had been the prizefighting champion of that country in his class for many years, was sitting on his porch one day, when a funeral procession came by. "Come here, Father," said he to his aged parent. "Come out on the porch and look down there. There goes the champion who has been defeated only once in the world's history: his name is Death, which Christ, by dying, slew."

In our text, our blessed Lord did three things:

> He abolished death; made it of none effect;
> He has brought life to light;
> He has wrought incorruptibility.

He death, by dying, slew (Heb. 2:14). For the soul redeemed by His precious blood, death has lost its sting. The believer has passed out of death into life (John 5:24). For him, death is behind; grace and glory lie before.

"Look!" said a nervous lady passenger to one of the sailors on the ship. "Look at that dark sky there; we're going to have a terrible storm." "Calm down, lady," said the salt, "that storm is behind us." So it is for the child of God. For the present, we have eternal life to live and enjoy. In the future, not only the soul, but the body, too, shall know the fulness of the blessing of the gospel of Christ won for us upon the Cross. This corruptible shall put on incorruption; our bodies shall be changed into His likeness!

# Two Deposits

*"For the which cause I also suffer these things: nevertheless I am not ashamed: for I know whom I have believed, and am persuaded that He is able to keep that which I have committed unto Him against that day.*

*"Hold fast the form of sound words, which thou hast heard of me, in faith and love which is in Christ Jesus. That good thing which was committed unto thee keep by the Holy Ghost which dwelleth in us."*

(2 Timothy 1:12-14)

That expression "committed unto" in verses 12 and 14 might well be translated by the word which all who ever do any banking will know quite well, the word "deposit". Paul says that he had made a deposit with God; and, also, that God had made a deposit with him. The one is seen in verse 12, and the other in verse 14.

In regard to Paul's committing himself and his possessions into God's bank, he has no reservations, for he can say, "I know Him, whom I have believed." Often we cannot say that we know "what, or when, or why, or whether, or which, or whither," but we can say we know Him, who is so worthy of our trust. We don't need to insist on collateral.

A Seminole Indian went into a bank in Miami, Florida to request a cash loan of some size. The banker explained to him that he could not do this unless the Indian had sufficient collateral. "What'um am collateral?" he asked. So, the banker explained to him that he would have to have something or other, either real estate, or a business of some kind, or perhaps cattle or horses, etc. The Indian readily proved to the man that he owned considerable property, so he got the loan.

Some months later, he came back and returned the cash, peeling off several thousand dollars from a tremendous bankroll big enough, as they say, to choke a horse. "Say," said the banker, "you ought not to carry all that money around with you; you might easily get robbed. Why don't you put it in our bank? We'll take care of it for you, and pay you interest, besides." The Indian looked at him suspiciously and said: "You got'um collateral?" He did not see why he should trust the banker any more than the banker had trusted him, with a good show of reason.

But Paul required no collateral from the Lord, though He has plenty. His bank will never burst; His capital resources are infinite. As the bank works with your money and pays you a dividend, so does our Lord. He works with, and multiplies, whatever you entrust to Him, and He will pay tremendous dividends in that day.

This heavenly banker is not like one down here that I heard about, who repeatedly and flatly refused a loan to a man who almost begged him to have pity on him. Finally, worn out by the man's persistence, he said: "Alright, on one condition! One of my eyes is an artificial one; no one ever guesses which one it is. If you can guess it, I will let you have the loan." Without hesitation, the suppliant said: "It is the right one." "Why, that's so, but what makes you so sure?" "That's easy," said the fellow. "I saw a gleam of mercy in it."

Not only does the believer make a deposit with God, but something has been committed to him. God does not demand any collateral from us, but He does look for faithfulness in the discharge of our responsibilities. It is the truth of God's Word that has been committed unto us to keep and use.

Paul was faithful in the discharge of his duty and could say: "I have kept the faith." I can trust the Lord; can He trust me? Sometimes even believers are seduced into the denial of the truth of God's precious Word. Young Christians, especially, are in danger of this as they go to college, where the Bible is often ridiculed. I have met, of recent years, several who lost their faith because they were led astray by the rantings of some cheap professor who knew no more about the Bible than a donkey. I have very often found that some, who make light of the Word of God, are like the fellows who bet one another that one could not say the Lord's prayer. They put up the money, and then the one repeated: "Now I lay me down to sleep; I pray the Lord my soul to keep." "Say," said the other, "I didn't think you knew it!" So, he let him have the money. That's about as much as the average person knows about the Bible. Let us, who love God's precious Word, hold fast and hold forth the Word of life.

# Rightly Dividing the Word

*"Study to shew thyself approved unto God, a workman that needeth not to be ashamed, rightly dividing the Word of truth."*

(2 Timothy 2:15)

This might well be the motto for everyone who seeks to be a servant of Christ. Such a one needs not only to have a good working knowledge of the Word of God, as our text suggests, but must apply its searching truth to himself before giving it out to others. That seems to be meant, in a measure, by the expression "rightly dividing the Word of truth". The idea is that we must face the Word fairly and not seek to get around it somehow.

Let's notice that the first word, "study", has no reference here to acquiring knowledge, which thought the English word would naturally suggest to our minds. The Greek word is translated in the New Testament by "be diligent", and means "to make haste", as it is translated in Luke 19:5, where Jesus urged Zacchaeus to make haste and come down; or it is found as "instantly" in Luke 7:4.

Also, the word "shew thyself" is found more frequently

under the verb "present", as in Romans 12:1, where the believer is told to present his body as a living sacrifice. It is also translated "yield" as in Romans 6:13, where we are told to yield ourselves unto God.

Thus, our text urges us to be in a hurry; to mean business; to present ourselves unto God; to yield ourselves - body, soul and spirit; to so live that God can approve of us; so to know His mind as to be able to handle His Word as workmen that need not to be ashamed of our deeds. We should earnestly present ourselves to Him, and say, as it were, like Isaiah: "Here am I; send me."

"Present thyself," says God. Note that "thyself". The Lord has only one like you, and you only have yourself as you are, so make the best of it. Yield yourself to Him.

A little girl asked her mother to please button up her dress for her. "Why don't you try to do things like that yourself?" said the mother. "Oh dear, oh dear," said the little miss, "what would I ever do without myself?" That's right, what would she? But even more important, what are you doing with yourself? Are you surrendering yourself and your substance to Him?

Perhaps you feel you are personally so insignificant; and you forget, perhaps, that a large company is made up of individuals, and each one is a necessary cog in the whole machinery.

Sometimes it pays to remember, as they say Bro. Spurgeon said once, that "a committee is a noun signifying many, but not signifying much!" If every Christian were like I am, what would the Church be like? This is a good question for each of us to ask ourselves.

Be a workman who knows how to use his tools. For the believer, that means, first of all, to get a thorough working knowledge of God's Word. A man never becomes a carpenter merely by learning the theory of building, but only by actually doing the work - by learning to use a saw and a hammer. First, we make the Word of God our own by studying it; then by practising it. Practise it in a Sunday School class, or at a mission, or by speaking to individuals in daily life, etc. Be a workman!

"Rightly dividing the Word of truth." This expression may mean, as we suggested before, facing the Word as it speaks to one's self, and permitting it to judge yourself and form your life in its light, so God can approve of it. It also, no doubt, has the idea the A V suggests: knowing how to rightly divide it, knowing who is addressed, what the subject in hand is, etc. One must learn to whom a particular thing is written, what its context is, etc.

A truth, perfectly suitable in its proper place, could be deadly error when taken out of its context, as for instance: A physician was giving a husband instructions over the phone in regard to his sick wife. The lines became crossed somehow, and the husband found himself listening to a boss explaining to one of his employees what to do in the case of a defective steamboiler. The husband heard something like this:

"Take a big sledge hammer and beat her good all around till you knock everything loose inside; then pour a gallon of kerosene inside of her, stuff her full with lots of old newspapers, and set her on fire."

That might be a good dose for an old boiler, I really don't know, but I know it is terrible advice for a poor sick woman. Many of the conclusions come to by uninstructed, would-be Bible teachers are only a little less ridiculous, or far more serious.

A context can give an entirely wrong thought, or correct a wrong thought. Sometimes it works like this: many years ago, I was walking down a street, when I saw three bushel baskets full of eggs in a grocery store window. On the basket at the right was a sign reading, "Strictly Fresh Eggs - 27 cents a dozen". The one on the left read, "Fresh Eggs - 23 cents a dozen"; while, on the other centre basket was the ominous sign, "Eggs - 19 cents a dozen". In this context, one could actually smell those eggs in the middle. Ordinarily, the word "eggs" sounds alright; but in that context, it smelled to high heaven.

Another important thing to note in Bible study is whether the language is literal or symbolical, which can make a lot of difference in the meaning. At Bible school, that was one question asked me as much as any other, and I always told the scholars that this was not easy to determine; one could only gain proficiency by getting intimately acquainted with the Word of God.

We speak in symbolic language every day, and the only way we know whether we are speaking literally or not is because, through the years, we get used to hearing such expressions. For instance, when one says, "Don't put all your eggs in one basket," you don't need to start looking around for chickens or eggs, because there aren't any around; it is a symbolic expression.

When a person says to you, "My, I'm blue this morning," he might look pale to you, and you look in vain for the blue. Or, when they say, "My head is spinning around," you won't see that phenomenon, either. All those and thousands more we use all the time; they are symbolic, and we only learn to know them as years go by.

When I first was in this country, I remember asking a motorman on a streetcar why we were moving so slowly. "Well, you see," said he, "the car that is ahead is behind." How about that? So, it is only through diligent search and careful observation that one becomes a workman who knows how to evaluate and communicate the Word of God.

# Scriptures

*"And that from a child thou hast known the Holy
Scriptures, which are able to make thee wise unto
salvation through faith which is in Christ Jesus. All
Scripture is given by inspiration of God, and is profitable
for doctrine, for reproof, for correction, for instruction in
righteousness."*

(2 Timothy 3:15-17)

The Bible claims for itself to be the Word of God - the
living Word, inbreathed by God Himself. When the Lord
God made Adam away back, He stooped over that inert
form, as it were, as it lay on the ground, breathed into his
nostrils the breath of life, and man became a living soul.
Even so, He breathed into His written Word His life-breath,
and the Bible became a living book (Heb. 4:12).

When you look at a dead thing or person, it looks the
same no matter how often you look, but a living being
changes its appearance constantly. Even so, the Word of God
ever presents new facets of beauty, power and love, because
it is a living Word. It is truly an inexhaustible treasure.

The Bible is called the Word of God some forty three
times.

It is also called the Word of truth. That's why so many
close their ears to it, because truth is so unpalatable to the
sinner. A dead gravestone will suffer the lie it advertises, for
someone has said that "an epitaph frequently is a
monumental lie", but the living Word of God tells the truth.

The Bible is also called the Word of life, in Philippians
2:16.

It is called the Word of faith, in Romans 10:8. God's truth,
bowed to by faith, imparts divine life to the believing soul.
Men often reject the voice of Scripture because its truth
hurts. It not only speaks of God's wondrous love, but shows
how very much sinful man needs that grace, and how
terrible is the result of rejecting Christ as Saviour. It speaks

of an eternity of weeping, wailing and gnashing of teeth.

Out West years ago, a young preacher assured his listeners that there was no hell. "God is love," said he, "and never will send anybody to eternal perdition." One day a delegation of rough cowboys came to see him and told him: "Sir, if there is no hell, we don't need you; and if there is, we don't want you!" That makes good sense.

Our text from 2 Timothy 3 makes the following points:

1. The Bible claims to be the Word of God.

2. It speaks with the Wisdom of God. It makes the soul wise unto salvation, as happened with Timothy, who heard God's truth from his childhood. It is a great blessing to hear the gospel in infancy, to have believing parents.

Preaching in missions through the years, my experience was that nearly all old sinners brought to Christ in Rescue Missions had heard the gospel in their childhood, or came from christian homes. This should be a great encouragement to those who work with children, teaching them the truths of God's precious Word.

3. The Bible shows the Way to God. The way to God is through faith in cChrist Jesus. Timothy was brought up in a godly home, as was I; but, like myself, there came a time when he had to choose for himself; a time when he turned to the Lord in repentance and in saving faith.

4. It teaches the Will of God. It tells us what is right (doctrine); it rebukes us when we don't do what is right (reproof); it shows us how to do the right (correction), and instructs us how to live right (instruction in righteousness).

5. It fits us for the Work of God, for it thoroughly furnishes the believer unto all good works.

# Final Advice

*"Preach the Word; be instant in season, out of season; reprove, rebuke, exhort with all longsuffering and doctrine. For the time will come when they will not endure sound doctrine; but after their own lusts shall they heap to themselves teachers, having itching ears;*

*"And they shall turn away their ears from the truth, and shall be turned unto fables. But watch thou in all things, endure afflictions, do the work of an evangelist, make full proof of thy ministry.*

*"For I am now ready to be offered, and the time of my departure is at hand."*

(2 Timothy 4:2-6)

The aged servant of Christ is about to depart for the glory to be with Christ, and so he urges his son Timothy to carry on the work, which was to continue for nineteen centuries, though Paul likely had no conception that the Lord would not return for that long period of time. But so it is, and his words to Timothy apply with equal force to us. We must carry on and must carry forth the Word of life, till Jesus comes again.

Paul had said long before that to depart and be with Christ was far better. He uses an expression that suggests a vessel, laden with precious cargo, leaving port for foreign shores. He thinks, as it were, of his death, not as the end but, rather, as the beginning of his journey - a journey that, for him and for us, too, will continue throughout all eternity. He expects to reach the Haven with a heavily-laden ship; to hear from the lips of his Lord the words, "Well done!" in warmest commendation. And so he tells us:

(1) To preach the Word - by life and by lip, which is open to all believers alike. It is said that the late Dr. Campbell

Morgan and his three sons, all ministers of the Word, were sitting together one day, when one of the sons raised the question of which of them was the best preacher. One of them said instantly, "Mother, of course!" Yes, we are all preachers.

(2) Be instant in season and out of season. "How many seasons are there in the year?" asked the day school teacher of her class. Said little Jake, raising his hand: "Two, teacher!" "Two?" "Yes, that's what my papa always says - dull and busy." We should always be at it, persistently persisting.

Like the salesman who finally got to see the president of a big corporation, just a short while before the tycoon intended to leave for home. "Young man, you should consider yourself lucky," said he. "I've turned at least ten salesmen away today." "Yes, I know," said the other. "I'm them."

The time will come, said Paul, when men with itching ears will turn a deaf ear to the truth, and I'm afraid we are living in that day. And yet, as Paul told Timothy, we are to carry the gospel still, to do the work of an evangelist. There's no room for drones in God's beehive.

Have you heard this tale? Out West, stage-coach passengers in one section of the country were sold first, second and third class tickets; but when it came time to leave, all of them piled into the same coach, with no apparent distinction. When one passenger objected to this treatment, the driver told him: "Hold your horses! You'll find out after a while where the difference in the price comes in." Later in the day, they came to a rough and very steep mountain trail, and the driver called out: "All first class passengers, keep your seats; all second class passengers, get out and walk; all third class passengers, get out and push!"

We are apt, naturally, to get discouraged because of the lack of interest in the Word in our day, but we should still press on. God is blessing in many places. We should, perhaps, be encouraged by the rooster's comment when he got back from a trip to the desert. He had come across an ostrich egg. Calling all his wives together, he took them out there to see it for themselves. Showing them the egg, he said: "Of course, I don't expect the impossible; but it just shows you what is being done in other places!"

Have you heard the tale of the two frogs who fell into a can of milk? In the morning, one was found dead at the bottom. But the other, who had thrashed around all night to keep on top of the milk, was sitting triumphantly on a large chunk of butter, the product of his energy!

# Threefold Salvation

*"In hope of eternal life, which God, that cannot lie, promised before the world began."*

(Titus 1:2)

*"Teaching us that, denying ungodliness and worldly lusts, we should live soberly, righteously, and godly, in this present world."*

(Titus 2:12)

*"That being justified by His grace, we should be made heirs according to the hope of eternal life."*

(Titus 3:7)

Threefold salvation is presented to us in the Epistle to Titus:

In the first chapter, the believer is seen as heavenborn; in the second, as heavenlike; and in the third, as heavenbound.

In the first chapter, it is his life in relation to other believers; in the second, in relation to himself; in the third, in relation to the world.

We see promise of life in chapter 1; performance in chapter 2, and prospect of life in chapter 3.

The commandment of God our Saviour - chapter 1:3.
The doctrine of God our Saviour - chapter 2:10.
The kindness and love of God our Saviour - chapter 3:4.

The epistle begins with the hope of eternal life, promised in eternity past by God to Himself (1:2). It ends with the hope of eternal life promised to us, for the eternity that lies ahead (3:7).

All this is very precious and has been brought to us, as chapter 1:3 tells us, through preaching. God, by His servants, through His Word, has told us about all this. And where God speaks, it pays for man to listen and keep his mouth shut. But there are many unruly and vain talkers, whose mouths must be stopped (1:10-11). Many folks like to hear themselves talk. They seldom stop to listen and, therefore, are so ignorant of the truth of God.

Many are like the old man, who was often heard to talk to himself. When asked why he did so, he replied: "For two reasons: I love to talk to a smart man, and I love to hear a smart man talk!"

Verses 9-16 of Titus 1 refer to talkers who ought to be listeners. They talk back, verse 9; they talk but say nothing (their talk is vain or empty), verse 10; they talk wrong things, which they ought not to say, verse 11; they speak lies, verse 12; and they talk as hypocrites, professing to be what they are not, verse 16.

Over against this sham, the true believer should be able to teach sound doctrine, verse 9; be sound in the faith, verse 13; and express himself in sound speech, chapter 2:8. This "sound" does not mean mere sound, as has often been said when a speaker finished and some listener commented that it was a sound message; but another replied, "Indeed it was, very sound; in fact, it was nothing but sound." This word "sound" does not mean noise, of course, but, rather, poise. It is meant to add to the health of the hearers, not to the wealth of the speaker. It is to be delivered, not for filthy lucre's sake, but for His glory.

# What Grace Teaches

*"For the grace of God that bringeth salvation hath appeared to all men, teaching us that, denying ungodliness and worldly lusts, we should live soberly, righteously, and godly, in this present world;*

*"Looking for that blessed hope, and the glorious appearing of the great God and our Saviour Jesus Christ;*

*"Who gave Himself for us, that He might redeem us from all iniquity, and purify unto Himself a peculiar people, zealous of good works."*

(Titus 2:11-14)

I might say that the first and the last verses of the above text form, as it were, the frame for the picture of verses 12 and 13. In the frame, we read of: (1) the grace of God, bringing salvation; (2) Christ's incarnation; (3) He gave Himself for us, thus propitiation; (4) redemption, for He came to redeem us; (5) sanctification, to purify unto Himself a special people; and (6) service, for we are to be zealous of good works.

Thus, in the frame, are six precious things our blessed Lord came to do for us. And, in the picture within the frame, verses 12-13, we see what we are to do for Him; we are to be learning, living, looking.

These are sandwiched in between His two appearances: His appearing nineteen centuries ago at His incarnation, when He came to be our Saviour; and His appearing in the future to display Himself and us to wondering worlds.

The grace of God is now our teacher. The Greek word for grace here is "Charis", or "Anne", in our language, so we might say that we believers have a gentle lady teacher named Anne, in contrast to under law, when the schoolmaster was a hard teacher, carrying a big stick.

The law said "thou shalt", but grace says "let us". It is not the law of God inspiring fear that constrains us, but the love of God which evokes devotion. It is by the power of love that henceforth we do not live unto ourselves, but unto Him.

We are going to God's school today, well equipped for further study and practice, for we have a B.A. Degree (born again) to start with.

Some, alas, are ever learning and never able to come to the knowledge of the truth (2 Timothy 3:7). I believe two main reasons account for such a state of soul: (1) the mind and heart are not open to honestly receive the Word because of pre-conceived notions or erroneous teaching; and (2) there is a lack of putting into practice what the Word of God demands. The grace of God here is said to teach two main lessons - what not to do, and what to do. To say "no" to ungodliness and worldly lusts, and to say "yes" to a life of holiness and righteousness.

Learning leads to living. As the mother said to her little boy when he asked, at the close of the minister's sermon: "Mom, is it all done now?" She replied, "No, son, it is all said now; now we must go out and do it." Live soberly, towards one's self; righteously, towards others; godly, towards God: inward, outward, and upward.

Learning, living, and then looking. Looking for that blessed hope - the hope of His coming for us to take us where He is; looking also for the appearing of His glory, when He shall come back to earth and we shall come with Him. Everyone that has this hope in Him purifies himself, even as He is pure.

In verse 14 we read of:
>    the Person - He gave *Himself*;
>    the Passion - He *gave* Himself;
>    the Purpose - that He might redeem us;
>    the Possession - to have us especially His own;
>    the Prize - to make us zealous of good works.

Thus, in verses 11 to 15 we have: salvation, verse 11; education, verse 12; anticipation, verse 13; sanctification, verse 14; and exhortation, verse 15.

# Past; Present; Future

*"For we ourselves also were sometimes foolish, disobedient, deceived, serving divers lusts and pleasures, living in malice and envy, hateful, and hating one another.*

*"But after that the kindness and love of God our Saviour toward man appeared, not by works of righteousness which we have done, but according to His mercy He saved us, by the washing of regeneration, and renewing of the Holy Ghost;*

*"Which He shed on us abundantly through Jesus Christ our Saviour; that being justified by His grace, we should be made heirs according to the hope of eternal life."*

(Titus 3:3-7)

Here again we have the past, the present and the future. In the past, the kindness and love of God our Saviour toward man appeared (the Greek word here is the word "philanthropy"); in the present we are saved and have the fulness of the Spirit; in the future lies the unfading inheritance which we shall share with our blessed Lord (Rom. 8:17).

Once we were foolish (did no sensible thinking of our own); we were disobedient (refused to hearken to God's thinking); we were deceived by the devil's thoughts. But His mercy saved us; His Word cleansed us; His Spirit renovated us. He did it all, and now it is our privilege to do His will.

Six times in Titus, the believer is reminded that this new life is to be seen in good works. Not in mere talking, as in 3:9, but in walking and working.

Avoid genealogies, we read. The natural man prides himself often on his ancestry, as the Jew was proud of his connection with the fathers of Israel, see Paul in Philippians 3:4-6. But, instead of boasting of one's family tree, the Christian boasts in the Cross (Gal. 6:14), the tree from which he traces all his blessings; the tree where Jesus died for him. His life does not flow from his forebears; it begins at death, at Calvary.

As far as our natural descent is concerned, we have nothing to be proud of. As someone said to an unbeliever, who claimed his descent from the ape: "I don't think any of my foreparents ever swung by the tail, but I have no doubt but that a few of them swung by the neck."

Man's father is Adam; his grandfather was dust, and his great-grandfather was nothing. One blueblood boasted: "My grandparents came over on the Mayflower." "They were lucky," was the reply, "the immigration laws are much stricter now."

No, the thing to praise God for is not where you came from, but where you are going; not the wealth you or your ancestors may have had once, but the glorious inheritance laid up for you in heaven is what counts; not to look back to your natural birth, but to your spiritual birth; not the family tree, but the tree where your Saviour hung.

The Cross, the Cross, oh, that's our gain,
For 'twas on that the Lamb was slain;
'Twas there, for us, the Saviour died;
'Twas there the Lord was crucified.

"What are your prospects, young man?" asked the prospective father-in-law. I don't know what the answer was, but it is wonderful when one can say that, thanks to the riches of God's grace, my prospects are just wonderful. I've been made an heir according to the hope of eternal life. The glory shines before me; all glory to His Name!

# Faith

*"Now faith is the substance of things hoped for, the evidence of things not seen."*

(Hebrews 11:1)

This verse tells us that, for the present, faith makes unseen things real and, for the future, it makes them sure. Often these two features combine for the joy and blessing of the believer.

I remember that, when our younger son, Carroll, was a boy of about four, he wrote to me, through his mother, that he wanted me to bring him a bag of coloured marbles when I got home from my trip. I promised to do so. In order that I might not forget, I bought them immediately and lugged them around with me for several months.

When I got home, it happened to be in the winter, with quite a bit of snow on the ground. The little fellow came rushing out of the house. He did not offer to kiss me as usual; he did not ask whether I had brought the marbles; no, he just shouted out, full of excitement: "Dad, give me those marbles!" I tell you, it gave me a wonderful thrill to see his absolute faith in me. Faith, to him, had made those marbles real all the while I was gone, and had filled his mind with perfect assurance of having them when I got back.

There are several things worth noting: (1) that faith is only justified when there is a promise given; (2) that faith is in a person, not in things; and (3) that faith gives perfect assurance (when that faith is in God), for human beings are so apt to fail, either forgetting or otherwise unable to carry out their promises.

Yes, faith is in a person. It is not, in God's things, so much what you believe as whom you believe, and this is illustrated in daily life. I spoke frequently to children, using this illustration:

I'd say: "Children, I have some things in my pocket which I bought in the store yesterday. I saw the storekeeper take them and put them into a paper bag. I took them out of the bag last night, and laid some of them on my dresser. This morning, I put some of them in my pocket, and yet I have never seen them."

"I don't believe that," said a boy on one occasion. "Alright, I'll show it to you." So, I took a peanut out of my pocket and said: "See, I've never seen it, for it is inside of the shell." "Oh yes, now I believe it," said the boy.

"No, now you don't believe it; now you see it. If you had believed me, you would have believed it."

So, if you believe God, you believe what God says, no matter how impossible it might seem to you. "Without faith, it is impossible to please Him." Believing will often prevent harm and bitter disappointment.

One of our children repeatedly tried to put his hand on the hot electric toaster, but we warned him that it was hot and that it would hurt. The trouble with these electric gadgets is that they don't look hot when they are hot, and so the little fellow saw no reason to believe us.

One day he managed to succeed in touching it, and the little infidel was cured in a moment. After that, he would not even come near to it when it was cold. Faith in God and in His Word saves the soul from hell and brings boundless blessing to the believer.

But we must remember that faith can only be in a revelation. Faith is not superstition; it is not something you can exercise without warrant. Faith, the faith we are speaking of, is faith in God, and God only reveals Himself to us in His Word, His promise. What God has promised, that He will perform (Rom. 4:21).

It is impossible to believe someone or something you have never heard; faith in God is in God's revelation of Himself. He has made us many and precious promises in His Word in regard to our present and future spiritual blessings; but when it comes to details in our daily life down here, we must generally say, with the Lord Jesus, "Thy will be done."

Years ago, a brother told me he had prayed for years that his wife, who was ill of a rare disease, might be healed by the Lord. Finally, when she got no better, he took her out West to go and see the famous faith healer, Amy McPherson. But his wife died ere he could take her there, from the exhaustion of the long journey.

"I can't understand," said he to me. "I have prayed for years in faith, and yet the Lord did not heal her. Can you explain this?" "Oh, yes, I believe I can. You did not pray in faith. That's the reason." "But I did," said he. "No, you didn't." With this, he got quite angry and said: "What do you know about it? I did pray in faith."

So, I sought to show him that faith can only be in God's promise, and that nowhere in Scripture does God ever unconditionally promise to heal those who are sick. In such cases, and in many other cases, one can only pray in the tenor of our Lord's words: "Father, not My will, but Thine be done." But where God's Word clearly promises us certain things, we can lay hold on them by faith in perfect assurance.

# Good and Perfect Gifts

*"Let no man say when he is tempted, I am tempted of God: for God cannot be tempted with evil, neither tempteth He any man: but every man is tempted, when he is drawn away of his own lust, and enticed.*

*"Then when lust hath conceived, it bringeth forth sin: and sin, when it is finished, bringeth forth death. Do not err, my beloved brethren.*

*"Every good gift and every perfect gift is from above, and cometh down from the Father of lights, with whom is no variableness, neither shadow of turning."*

(James 1:13-17)

The natural man likes to blame God for his troubles, and to take credit for what he considers the good in his life. But he must learn that the good all comes from above, and the evil comes from within and from around.

Years ago, I was painting a gospel text on a trailer, when I suddenly heard a voice behind me, saying: "Do you believe in that old fashioned stuff? Not me; I threw it all overboard when I was nine years old. I came from Sunday School one day and said to my mother: 'Mother, did God make me?' and she said 'Yes'.

'Well, then, I'm through with God forever'; and I have gotten along without Him ever since. I don't believe in God or in the Bible." "What makes you so bitter?" said I, looking puzzled. "I'll tell you." With this, he turned around and showed me an ugly red hole where his right ear should have been. "You see that?" said he, "that's the kind of an ear God gave me, when He gives others two good ears."

Man likes to blame his troubles on God or on the devil; he is always looking for a substitute sinner, when he ought to turn in faith and humility to God's substitute Saviour.

Don't blame the devil for your troubles, either. Our text says that "man is drawn away of his own lust". Even Eve could not blame her fall on Satan. When the devil tempted her, he found her already at the forbidden tree; she had already sinned in heart before she did it in deed. What business did she have at that spot? Satan merely gave her a push in the direction she herself wanted to travel.

"All good giving (as this might well read) and every perfect gift comes from above." God not only gives good gifts, but knows how to give them. Sometimes gifts may be good, yet not good for the particular person to whom they are given. Or again, we may give things to folks because we know they want them, when they would be much better off without - like giving a sharp knife to a small boy.

A lady, travelling by train, with her little girl in the charge of a nurse, was annoyed by the child's restlessness and frequent crying. She told the nurse to keep her quieter. Shortly the child whined again, and the lady, sitting ahead, irritably asked the nurse what the child wanted now. "Oh, there is just something here she wants," said the nurse. "Well, let her have it," said the lady, "and keep her still!" After a few moments, the child really let out a fearful yell. "What's the trouble now? Didn't I tell you to let her have what she wants?" "She's got it," came the unexpected reply. It was a wasp on the windowsill which the child wanted.

God in His mercy knows when and how to give to us. But sometimes, when we are fretful like this child, He may let us have what we want, to teach us that we didn't want it; to teach us that He knows best.

He is the "Father of lights, with whom is no variableness, neither shadow of turning". Many of the heavenly lights are fixed, and there is no such thing as passing them, which, I understand, is the meaning of that phrase "no variableness". Others move in their orbit, and they never turn back (except as in the special case of King Hezekiah). So God, the Father of lights, neither goes back on His Word nor beyond His promises, and we cannot get beyond His love and care.

One dark night in the Bahamas, the master of a sailboat handed the wheel over to his mate and told him to "steer straight for that star there in the north", while he took a much needed rest. After some time, he woke up and could tell, by the motion of the boat, that they were headed in the wrong direction.

He ran up on deck and saw the north star behind them, instead of ahead. The black helmsman had just awakened and, seeing the star in the wrong place, said: "Boss, you better give me another star; I done steered past that one!"

But, praise God, we cannot get beyond His love and His power!

# Beneficial Exhortations

*"Of His own will begat He us with the Word of truth, that we should be a kind of firstfruits of His creatures. Wherefore, my beloved brethren, let every man be swift to hear, slow to speak, slow to wrath:*

*"For the wrath of man worketh not the righteousness of God. Wherefore lay apart all filthiness and superfluity of naughtiness, and receive with meekness the engrafted Word, which is able to save your souls."*

(James 1:18-21)

"Of His own will begat He us with the Word of truth." Through man's will, he became a sinner; through God's will, he becomes saved. And God begets the soul that trusts Him through the Word of truth, in contrast to the lie by which Satan led Eve astray.

Thus, believers become the firstfruits of His creatures. Adam and Eve were the firstfruits of the old creation back there in Eden, but sin spoiled all that. But our verse seems to indicate that, from all eternity, God intended that man, redeemed through Christ, should be His real, true creation; we are the firstfruits of the new creation.

Adam and Eve, typical of Christ and the Church, were a total failure, but Christ, having loved the Church and given Himself for her, now takes her up into perfect fellowship with Himself, into a union that can never fail.

After his practical manner, James, led by the Spirit, now urges us, His new creatures, to act accordingly. So, be swift to hear, slow to speak, slow to wrath. Eve practised the reverse; she was slow to listen to God, and altogether too swift to talk. Swift to hear; that's advice worth heeding. We need to know God's mind.

Oftentimes, some folks want me to come over and explain something to them from the Word, but when I get there, I find that they do all the talking. One husband said, "My wife is a very outspoken woman." "By whom?" was the cryptic answer.

God's Word says that we should be swift to hear and slow to speak. Someone has said: "Remember, when you're talkin', you ain't learnin' nothin'!" Let your walk stop your talk! "Let your light so shine before men, that they may see your good works, and glorify your Father which is in heaven" (Matt. 5:16). Be swift to hear, as God is, for "Before they call, I will answer, and while they are yet speaking, I will hear." Be slow to speak, for God is, since He has been silent now for over 1900 years. Perhaps soon He will speak again, with a voice that shall shake heaven and earth (Heb. 12:26). Be slow to wrath, even as God is, for "the Lord is merciful and gracious, slow to anger and plenteous in mercy" (Psalm 103:8).

Lay aside all filthiness (moral evil) and naughtiness (spiritual evil) and receive with meekness the engrafted Word. There is a steady development in christian life, as seen in the growth of a graft in a tree. The new divine life develops, while the old life is cut away. John the Baptist laid the axe to the root of the tree. He did not tear the root out of the ground, but left it there.

I am the same person I was before my conversion, but a shoot of divine life was implanted at my conversion. As the new life develops (through feeding on the Word), the old stock is cut down, and bye and bye the old tree bears new fruit, through the divine life within, empowered by the Holy Spirit. Old suckers will constantly spring up and need to be cut down (severely dealt with in self judgment), so that the life of Christ may have its way.

# Word as a Mirror

*"But be ye doers of the Word, and not hearers only, deceiving your own selves. For if any be a hearer of the Word, and not a doer, he is like unto a man beholding his natural face in a glass: for he beholdeth himself, and goeth his way, and straightway forgetteth what manner of man he was.*

*"But whoso looketh into the perfect law of liberty, and continueth therein, he being not a forgetful hearer, but a doer of the work, this man shall be blessed in his deed."*

(James 1:22-25)

The apostle likens the Word of God here to a looking glass, which is one of the most striking figures used. Others, as you know, are fire, a hammer, a sword, a lamp, etc. A mirror has such a gentle, gracious, and yet faithful way of telling the truth. It does not scream at you or hit you with a club; yet it can make you feel most uncomfortable. Also, it normally speaks to each one individually, telling the truth without embarrassing you before others.

So it is with the Word of God. Instead of looking into the Word, man often looks at his fellowmen and measures himself by what he sees there, thus coming to wrong conclusions and leading to much confusion.

For instance, two men were doing a job together. When they were through, one man, who was clean, went and washed his face, while the other, whose face was dirty, did not wash up. The reason for this was that they looked at each other, instead of in the mirror. The clean-faced man, looking at the one with the dirty face, decided that his own face probably was dirty, too, so he washed; but the dirty-faced one, seeing the other so clean, thought he must have been clean, too, so he didn't bother to wash.

Had they but looked into a looking glass, the truth would have set them straight. Even so, sinners look at each other, and so, many think they are alright because they look as good as their neighbours. The Word of God would have shown them that they all were filthy in God's sight and badly needed cleaning up.

It says in our text that a man beholds his natural face in a glass. This word is literally "the face of his birth". Someone said he could say for sure that he was not two-faced, for if he were, he would use the other one!

The man who is only a hearer of the Word of God and not a doer is he who beholds his face in a glass and straightway forgets what manner of man he is. Now, who is it that runs off right after seeing his/her picture in a looking glass? It is the homely, the ugly one, isn't it? A girl or man with lovely features just delights to dawdle in front of the mirror. Hence, if the person looks and then goes away, it proves such an one does not like what he sees in the mirror.

That's the very reason folks turn from the Word of God. It tells them the truth in a most uncompromising manner - that they are ugly in His sight; that they are lost sinners, helpless and bound for hell, and, of course, they don't like it.

The Word of God, as a mirror, goes deeper than an ordinary one; it reveals what's on the inside and not merely the outside, for God looketh on the heart.

A black girl in a store asked for a pair of flesh-coloured stockings, and the clerk, thinking to be funny, threw a black pair on the counter. The customer picked them up and threw them down again, exclaiming: "Those aren't flesh colour; they're skin colour!" And, of course, she was right.

If you skin a white, yellow, red, or black person, I can tell you what they would all look like: they'd all be ugly and repulsive; and that's how the natural man looks in the sight of God. You can read one such description in Isaiah 1:5-6. Man naturally resents this blunt view of him.

I am reminded of the gentleman who had his picture taken by a commercial photographer. He was anything but handsome. When he came for the pictures, he refused to take them or pay for them, saying: "They are terrible! They don't even look like me! Nobody would know that was me!" So he left in a huff.

Then the photographer took one of the finished pictures and put it in his showcase, right by the main street, with this caption: "This is the picture of the worst cheat in town." It wasn't long before the man was back in a rage, demanding to know what he meant by holding him up to public ridicule in that way.

"Why should you care?" was the answer. "You told me yourself that nobody would know by this picture that it was you; nobody will know it's you." He paid for the pictures fast enough to get his face out of the showcase. The trouble was, of course, that the pictures looked too much like him!

Then, too, there are many who get angry with the preacher and reject the Word of God because it shows them what they really are. For instance, here is a man driving along, when he suddenly hears the sickening sound of a police siren behind him, and he is moved over to the kerb. In addition to the lecture received, insult is added to injury by the ticket the cop gives him.

After the officer leaves, he takes a monkey wrench and smashes the speedometer, saying: "Why did you have to go 70 miles an hour?" Does he? Of course not.

Yes, that's exactly the reaction man has toward God's Word. The Word does not make man a sinner; it just tells him that he is one. The speedometer does not make the driver exceed the speed limit; it warns him that he is doing so, and warns him of the consequences, but he pays no heed.

Don't find fault with the Bible. It is faithfully showing you what you are, warning you of the results of disobedience, and pointing you to the divine remedy, found in the precious atoning sacrifice of Christ.

There are many who, when they hear the Word preached, feel how well this applies to somebody else they know. They say: "That just suits so-and-so; too bad he isn't here to hear this." As one old preacher said: "Many folks die in their sins from too much generosity. They give the sermon away to everybody else and keep none for themselves!"

I read once that a seedy old fellow with a long, matted beard found a piece of mirror one day and, looking into it, said: "Say, I didn't know that my old grandpa ever had his picture took!" Coming home, he laid the glass on the window sill, and when he had gone out, his wife saw it. Looking into it, she exclaimed: "So that's the old hag he's always talking to on the corner!" Both of them saw someone else in the mirror, and that's a real failing among humans.

Then, of course, there are ever so many who are brought into touch with the truth - who see themselves there and realize they don't look good enough even to suit themselves. So they start to doll themselves up; to try and fit themselves and make themselves acceptable in His sight.

I see this illustrated so often. I am riding on a train or in a plane. A young lady sits opposite me or a little ahead. She has scarcely settled herself before she starts digging around in one of those big handbags ladies carry, and out comes a mirror. She looks at herself from all angles and curves, and apparently does not like her looks, for she starts rummaging some more in that bag, and brings out lipstick, powder, etc. I thought she looked pretty nice, but not she. She forthwith begins to repair the shortcomings her critical eye discovers.

So it is with the sinner. Somehow many feel they are not what they should be, so they start to turn over new leaves; they join the church; they clean up the outside. They forget that only the blood of Jesus Christ can cleanse from all sin; that God alone can purify the inside. Only He can make the heart clean, and will do so, once that person commits his/her soul to Him in faith.

But, praise God, there are many who not only look into the Word, but continue looking therein, and thus become not merely hearers, but also doers of the word. Once having looked into the mirror and having seen one's sinful condition there, and having turned in faith to Christ for salvation, the believer continues looking into the Word.

Not now a passing glance, and then forgetting the unpalatable truth of one's guilty estate, but now continuing to look, and seeing in the mirror of the Word not merely one's own description as a sinner, but now also seeing the face of Jesus Christ reflected there, and all the glory of God shining forth from that lovely face (2 Cor. 4:6).

The believer sees Christ in the Scriptures, and delights to see Him and learn to know Him better every day. I have continued looking into the Word now for almost 60 years, and my soul has thrilled all those years in seeing the beauty of the Lord, of Him who is the fulness of the Godhead.

This mirror of the Word is spoken of under a striking title: the perfect law of liberty. Sounds sort of paradoxical, doesn't it? We don't think of law in connection with liberty; yet such it is. Though we are redeemed, set free, forgiven, we are still subject to law, for, as Paul says in 1 Corinthians 9:21: "We are not without law to God, but under the law to Christ."

This is a new law; not the legal code of the Old Testament, but the new law of love, as Jesus said: "If ye love Me, keep My commandments."

When two people are married, they immediately are bound by new laws. The law of love demands that, henceforth, they should live for each other, as they say in the wedding ritual: "leaving all others, cleave only to her and to him". It has been said that in the word "wedding", we comes before I.

Once Christ has won the heart, love becomes the motivating force for pleasing Him, and this law of love is a bondage that is yet, at the same time, true liberty to the soul that loves Him. The Word of God becomes, to the believer, the law of liberty.

# The Tongue

*"Behold also the ships, which though they be so great, and are driven of fierce winds, yet are they turned about with a very small helm, whithersoever the governor listeth. Even so the tongue is a little member, and boasteth great things. Behold, how great a matter a little fire kindleth!*

*"And the tongue is a fire, a world of iniquity: so is the tongue among our members, that it defileth the whole body, and setteth on fire the course of nature; and it is set on fire of hell.*

*"For every kind of beasts, and of birds, and of serpents, and of things in the sea, is tamed, and hath been tamed of mankind: but the tongue can no man tame; it is an unruly evil, full of deadly poison.*

*"Therewith bless we God, even the Father; and therewith curse we men, which are made after the similitude of God. Out of the same mouth proceedeth blessing and cursing. My brethren, these things ought not so to be.*

*"Doth a fountain send forth at the same place sweet water and bitter? Can the fig tree, my brethren, bear olive berries? Either a vine, figs? So can no fountain both yield salt water and fresh."*

(James 3:4-12)

The tongue! Here, as has often been said, is a subject that is in everybody's mouth. It is likened, among other similes, to the helm of a ship, suggesting that the tongue needs to be controlled by a strong and steady hand. If a ship started out on a voyage with no hand on the wheel, it would ere long go to smash somewhere. So also the soul that goes through life without Christ, the Captain of salvation.

We all ride around in those contraptions called automobiles, a word which means "self-moving". But we all know they don't move themselves; and when occasionally they do (running away on a steep street when someone has left the brakes off or something like that), what damage they can cause to themselves and to people! An automobile needs a hand on the wheel; an intelligent person is needed to guide and control it.

I said "an intelligent person", for it has been said that, in many cases, the most dangerous part of a car is the nut that holds the steering wheel!

For our soul's eternal welfare, we need the sure and powerful hand of our blessed Lord upon us; and about the first thing He does is to take control of our tongue, likened here to the rudder of a vessel.

There is a beautiful picture of this on Calvary. That dying thief, who a while previously had derided the Lord Jesus, turned in repentance to Him. That criminal was nailed hands and feet. If salvation depended on his going somewhere, it was too late, for his feet were nailed. If it depended on his doing something, it was too late for that also, for his hands were nailed.

But his heart was not nailed; it was still beating. And his tongue was still free, and so it is those two members of his body that he used, to the salvation of his soul. I am sure the Lord, by the Spirit, took control of that tongue, to utter these words: "Lord, remember me when Thou comest into Thy kingdom!"

Romans 10:9 says that, with the heart, man believes; and, with the mouth, confession is made unto salvation; and it is in that manner the dying thief was saved. Those lips, till then often filled with vile language, even used to mock the Son of God, were now used to own Him as Lord and King. How wonderful it is to feel His hand on the helm of your soul!

The tongue, we are told, is naturally an unruly evil, a world of iniquity, wilder than the wildest animal. In the very construction of our bodies, we have a parable of this truth. For God has given us but one tongue, though we have two ears. We are to do twice as much listening as talking, at least. He has put the ears on the outside, where we can catch everything that comes along - one on one side of the head, and one on the other, so that, if we miss something at one side, we can catch it on the other.

But He has put the tongue away on the inside. The ears are made so that we can't close them; we always have to listen, whether we want to or not. But the tongue is put away inside a cavern - the mouth, shut away in what should be an ideal hiding place. Then, God has tied the tongue at one end. Just suppose He had tied it in the middle, and both ends could have wagged; what a tragedy that would have been!

Not only do we have but one tongue - inside, tied down, hidden from sight; but, in addition, God has put two fences in front of it - the teeth and the lips. Those teeth are there so you can bite the end of your tongue when you are tempted to say something nasty. That's what those teeth are for!

I believe I can prove that, for until a child starts to talk, it doesn't have any teeth, so evidently the teeth just come in time to stop rash words. Even all those precautions are not sufficient, for there are the lips as a second safeguard. But even that is not enough to ensure control, and so the psalmist prays, and we should, too: "Set a watch, O Lord, before my mouth; keep the door of my lips." (Psalm 141:3).

While the Lord does not give us another tongue when we get saved, He does put within us another heart. Ecclesiastes 10:2 says that "a wise man's heart is at his right, but a fool's heart is at his left".

There is a new source of life in the believer. As James here says: "Out of the same mouth proceedeth blessing and cursing", but he shows that they do not come out of the same source of supply, for a fountain cannot yield sweet water and bitter at the same time. If both come out of the same mouth at times, they do not come from the same source. The believer's makeup is something like the modern plumbing in our bathrooms. Both hot water and cold water come out of the same spout, but they do not come out of the same pipes.

A believer has a new heart within, a new life; and from this heart should come, by way of the tongue, words that are indicative of the new life within. As, once, evil communications proceeded out of our mouth, so now there should be words good to edifying.

Naturally, the tongue can be, and often is, a fearful evil; but, by the grace of God, it can become a powerful tool for good. To make sure that it is just that, we must yield its control into His hands. He must be the Captain who holds the helm of our ship.

# Christian's Future

*"Go to now, ye that say, Today or tomorrow we will go into such a city, and continue there a year, and buy and sell, and get gain: Whereas ye know not what shall be on the morrow. For what is your life? It is even a vapour, that appeareth for a little time, and then vanisheth away."*

(James 4:13-14)

Ye know not what shall be on the morrow. What a great mercy this is, that God has veiled the future from our eyes. We know, through the many prophecies in the Word of God, a good deal about the future, but not about the immediate future, only the ultimate.

We believers know that the glory lies before us, an eternal inheritance with Christ in heaven. We know a good deal about the fearful judgments that shall sweep over this world, but we know nothing about what will happen tomorrow or the day after tomorrow. God has kindly hidden this from us.

Of course, we'd often love to know what will happen a few years ahead. Many a person, if he only could have foreseen developments, could have invested a few dollars in real estate somewhere and become a multi-millionaire almost overnight. If our foresight were as good as our hindsight, we might all be rich in earthly goods. However, that again might be the worst possible thing to happen to us, for, as one servant of Christ once said: "For every believer who goes astray on account of adversity, twenty go astray because of prosperity."

On the other hand, we may be deeply thankful we don't know the trials and afflictions the future may hold for us. I was walking down a city street some years ago, when, as I was passing a tiny cubbyhole store, I was accosted by a woman dressed like a gypsy, though her accent betrayed that she came from Brooklyn.

"I'll tell you your fortune," she said. I replied, "No, thank you; I know what it is to the last cent. I counted it this morning before I left home. It is just $3.48." "Oh," said she, "I don't mean that; I mean your future." "No, thank you, for several reasons. First of all, I don't believe you know it. Secondly, I don't want to pay your fee; and thirdly, and most important, if I thought you really knew it, I'd pay you every cent I've got to keep your mouth shut.

"I know my fortune as far as my future is concerned. I know I am going to see the Lord who died for me, and I am going to live with Him forever. But I don't know, and I don't want to know, my future here on earth, between now and then. If I had known, the day I got married, my life's future here on earth during the last 51 years, I would have died of heart failure on the spot! Praise God, I don't know my future down here."

Praise His Name, He bids us to live one day at a time. He tells us to take no anxious thought for the morrow, for the morrow will take care of the things of itself; sufficient unto the day is the evil thereof. Praise God, the sorrows and joys alike come in homeopathic doses, and thus contribute to real spiritual health and blessing. All I want is to live so as to utilize my time and talents, so that I shall not be ashamed before Him at His coming; to remember that time is short, like a vapour that passes away; to remember that which was said about a little one-horse town:

The city fathers decided to make the main street a one-way street. However, the trouble was that, when the folks left the town by this street, there was no way to get back into it, for it had only one street.

That's the way it is with life. "So teach us to number our days, that we may apply our hearts unto wisdom" (Psalm 90:12). Now, how do you number your days when you don't know how many you still have coming to you? You can't, and so I think we'll take the meaning of the Hebrew word "number" in Psalm 90 as meaning "appoint, or prepare".

In Jonah, we read that the Lord prepared a great fish, prepared a gourd, a worm, and an east wind. Each time, the Hebrew word is the same as "number" in Psalm 90. We are to prepare our days and use them wisely, to the best of our ability. Soon time may have flown by, and our days of living for Christ and serving Him down here will be over.

There is work to do - buy and sell and get gain, as our text said. Only, of course, we are to trade not merely for earthly gains, but in the service of our Lord. This is the time to be busy; not to be wishing for fishing, so to speak.

Like the pilot who flew over his old home village and looked down on the old creek. "When I was a youngster," he said, "I'd look up and see the planes fly overhead, while I sat by the creek fishing; and I wished I could be a pilot and fly a plane, too. Now I am flying a plane, and I wish I could sit down there by the old fishing hole and fish!"

Wishing and fishing were perhaps alright for the little boy, but not for the pilot. There is work to do. No fishing and wishing, but flying and trying. Buy and sell and get gain. Lay up blessing for eternity; don't just live for self.

A farmer rented out a few acres of land to a poor neighbour, with the understanding that he was to have a fourth of the crop for his share. When the corn was harvested, the renter took it all. When the owner of the land protested, he told him: "There was no fourth; there were only three wagonloads!"

# Christian Demeanour

*"Likewise, ye wives, be in subjection to your own husbands; that, if any obey not the Word, they also may without the Word be won by the conversation of the wives; while they behold your chaste conversation coupled with fear.*

*" Whose adorning let it not be that outward adorning of plaiting the hair, and of wearing of gold, or of putting on of apparel; but let it be the hidden man of the heart, in that which is not corruptible, even the ornament of a meek and quiet spirit, which is in the sight of God of great price."*

*"Likewise, ye husbands, dwell with them according to knowledge, giving honour unto the wife, as unto the weaker vessel, and as being heirs together of the grace of life; that your prayers be not hindered."*

(1 Peter 3:1-4, 7)

There is no need for christian women to go to a psychiatrist or a sociologist for advice in marital problems; they (or the husbands, too) need only to go to the Word, and the advice is free, effective and wholesome.

"Be subject to your husband" may not be palatable, but it is still a most excellent cure for unhappiness in the home. In the case where a sister in Christ is bound to an unsaved partner, if he is not won by the Word of God, he may be won by no word from his wife. The conversation of the wife, by which he is to be won for Christ, is not her talk, but her walk. The word "conversation" means behaviour or conduct.

For life is much more potent than the lip in this case. It is terribly possible to talk a husband away from Christ, rather than to win him for the Lord. You can give him a piece of your mind so often that he loses his, and the wife will have but little left of hers!

God's salvation is wonderful indeed, and the way to win

anyone to experience its blessedness often lies in making it attractive to the beholder. As one firm advertised, "Since we can't improve the product, we improve the box!" Folks often buy goods, not by their merit, but because they are so beautifully packaged. Salvation and the package it should come in are both so important.

In natural life, the male birds usually wear the gorgeous clothes, while the females dress in drab browns or greys. I believe there is a wise reason why God so ordered it. The female, in her colourless dress, draws very little attention, which is a protection against marauders who would steal the eggs she has laid, or kill the young ones she cares for. Her dull colouring is a protection against hunters and thieves.

In human life, however, the female loves to dress in gorgeous colours, for the simple reason that now she is the huntress and not the hunted; she is after the prey now. It has been said there are millions of reasons why women dress so attractively, and every one of them is a man.

Years ago, a man with powder in his horn
Went forth to hunt a deer;
But now a dear with powder on her nose
Goes forth to hunt a man.

Her "world", for that is the Greek word here translated "adorning", centres about plaiting the hair, wearing of gold and putting on of apparel. Those are her beauty treatments, for the word for world, "kosmos", has the idea of beauty. We get the word "cosmetics" from it.

There is nothing wrong with a woman's looking her best. Our text warns against overdoing it, making it the main object in life. This is clear when we read of "let it not be...of putting on of apparel". This could not mean in an absolute sense, for then it would say that a woman should wear no clothes at all. It evidently means that she must not overdress, as it says in 1 Timothy 2 (with modest apparel). The same is true in regard to fixing the hair or wearing gold or ornaments. Every Christian instinctively feels this is done when he sees a lady all rings, paint and powder.

It is right for a christian woman to look attractive in the sight of her husband, but she must remember that she has another "Man" to please even more. He loves to see inner beauty, for God looks on the heart. Yet I believe He loves to see outer beauty, too, or He would not have created it.

A christian woman should look well outwardly, but should even more cultivate beauty of character. A sensible young man will look for that inner beauty even more than for beauty of face or form.

Mr. Spurgeon used to tell young men not to propose to a girl when he saw her on Lord's days in church, but to visit her in her home on Saturdays, and see how she acted and looked in real everyday life.

Every married sister in Christ should be in love with two men; and this would not create an evil triangle, either. Her husband, one; the Lord Jesus, the other. The one she sees, and he sees her every day; the other, the One who looks on the heart, and in whose sight a meek and quiet spirit is of great price. He highly values this moral and spiritual comeliness.

Every christian woman should love her husband, and look as sweet in his eyes as possible; but she should love even more that "hidden Man of the heart", and dress for Him in that garment of lowliness and gentleness, which is precious to Him, and which magnifies Him in the eyes of others.

Romance often turns into regret when, after having been married a while, the wife does not seem to care any longer how she looks; she often looks in the morning like something the cat dragged in. Keep the outer self neat, as the frosting on your sweetness of disposition, and love will thrive. Our blessed Lord desires all of us to dress well within; and if we do, we will appreciate His love towards us more. It will be growing ever sweeter.

There is a word for husbands, too, but not very much. Perhaps it is because you can't tell them much. Just one verse: Treat your wife with honour and respect. Tell her often that you love her still. Don't bring home the bacon only; bring some applesauce, too, once in a while. She is the weaker vessel, reminding the husband that he is weak, too, and for this they both need prayer.

There is a special grace in this verse for married folks. It is called, in verse 7, the grace of life. God knows how much two, who live together, need special grace each day; and so He has made it available. Grace, that your prayers be not hindered. Two people closely in touch with each other are apt to get on each other's nerves.

As one man said, when he and his wife had a quarrel, she would generally become historical. "You mean hysterical?" asked his friend. "No, I mean historical. She brings up all the troubles of the past!"

For those times of trouble, grace is needed. There is this grace of life, it says here, that your prayers be not hindered. This seems to suggest that man and wife should pray together, facing their problems together before the throne of grace. Grudges and ill feelings will vanish when a husband and his wife kneel together at the close of the day to unburden their hearts in His presence, there where His grace is more than sufficient for every need.

# Baptismal Regeneration

*"By which also He (Christ) went and preached unto the spirits in prison; which sometime were disobedient, when once the longsuffering of God waited in the days of Noah, while the ark was a preparing, wherein few, that is, eight souls were saved by water.*

*"The like figure whereunto even baptism doth also now save us (not the putting away of the filth of the flesh, but the answer of a good conscience toward God,) by the resurrection of Jesus Christ."*

(1 Peter 3:19-21)

Years ago, I preached in a certain chapel on the text, "The blood of Jesus Christ His Son cleanseth us from all sin." At the close of the service, two young men, who had been sitting at the back of the room, spoke to me and told me they did not agree with what I had said.

They said that the blood of Christ shed on the Cross was not sufficient to save the soul; that one could not be saved except by being baptized in water; and that, too, preferably should be by a Mormon elder.

I asked them where they found in Scripture where baptism had anything to do with the salvation of the soul, and they called my attention to the above text. "You see," said they, "these people were saved by water, and the text says that, so now baptism also saves us."

"Well, then, will you please tell me who were baptized in Noah's day - the people who were saved or those who were lost? Not a drop of water touched the saved ones, but the baptized ones were all drowned and lost." They looked at each other, nonplussed, and one of them said: "What does it mean, then, when it says they were saved by water?"

"The answer is that it means just what it says; but it does not mean what you were trying to make out of it. Noah and his family were saved by water, but not by the water that fell on them, for none did. They were saved by the water that fell on the ark, and the ark is a type of Christ, even as the other two arks mentioned in the Bible - Moses' ark of Exodus 2:3, and the ark of the covenant.

"That water was water of doom, of judgment, for it drowned all those on the outside. So Christ was deluged by the waters of judgment when He hung on the Cross. All God's waves and billows rolled over Him; and, as a result, all those who are in Christ are safe forever. It is the waters of judgment that fell on Christ which saves the believer. But, only by faith is he safe in Christ (Rom. 8:1).

"Those outside were baptized and perished. It is to be feared that millions who trust in that baptism, but have never sheltered in Christ by faith, will perish in spite of, and while trusting in, their baptism."

The ark rose victoriously upon the waves, because it was built to stand the storm; it was pitched within and without with pitch. That "pitch" is the same word translated "atone", and speaks of His precious atoning blood. It is that which shelters the soul who hides in Christ from the judgment he so richly deserves.

Are you in Christ or out? That is the question. You may think that those who are saved by the grace of God are in the small minority. It seemed that way in Noah's day because only eight entered the ark; but when those eight came out, they were in the majority, for all the others had disappeared.

It will be so in the future, after the judgment of God has obliterated sinners from God's creation and has banished them to the blackness of darkness, where they will be invisible forever.

# Word of Life

*"That which was from the beginning, which we have heard, which we have seen with our eyes, which we have looked upon, and our hands have handled, of the Word of life."*

(1 John 1:1)

The Word of life: as John 1:14 tells us, the Word became flesh. Not God became flesh, for God never became anything; He always was and will be. But the Word became flesh. Christ was heard from away back, for all creation speaks with His voice.

As Psalm 19 tells us, "The heavens declare the glory of God; and the firmament sheweth His handywork. Day unto day uttereth speech, and night unto night sheweth knowledge. There is no speech nor language, where their voice is not heard." But when Christ came into the world, the Word was not only heard, but seen. The invisible became visible. We have this double feature in our Bible, too, for when we hear it, we hear the Word; when we read it, we see it.

First, as I have said, we hear the Word, for the world was created by the Word of God (Heb. 11:3). Christ is the author of creation (Col. 1:16). Second, as in our text, the Word was seen by the eyes of the apostles. Third, it was looked upon; and, fourth, it was handled.

We do the same four things (or should, at least) with Christ the written Word. We hear God's Word when it is read to us or we hear it preached; we see it next, as we read the Word for ourselves and as, by faith, Christ becomes a living reality to us, as Jesus said: "He that hath seen Me hath seen the Father." We see Jesus today by faith.

Next, we look upon Him, which suggests a closer scrutiny than in mere seeing. We look upon Him as we study and meditate upon God's Word. The precious things concerning

Christ do not lie upon the surface, but must be digged for. When we do dig, our reward will be even greater than that of the Arab of whom this tale is told:

As he was travelling with others, they encamped one night by a dry river bed. This man had a dream and heard a voice saying to him: "When you leave in the morning, take some pebbles and put them in your pocket; you'll be both glad and sorry you did." So, in the morning, he took a handful and put them in the pocket of his robe.

The next night, as they camped again, he recalled his dream and taking the pebbles; so he put his hand in his pocket and, to his amazement, the pebbles had turned into glittering diamonds. Then he realized the force of the words he had heard in his dream: "You'll be both glad and sorry you did." He was glad he took some, and sorry he didn't take more. Even so will it be with us when we fail to dig for God's hidden treasure trove; when we fail to lay up the riches of God's grace and love.

Finally, we are to handle the Word of life. Not alone to enjoy it for ourselves, but to learn to share its glories and joys with others. The more we use it, the more valuable it becomes to us, we'll find.

Not like the city family who rented a home in the country for the summer. Having quite a bit of garbage to dispose of, they conceived the idea of buying a little pig and feeding it the offal. When they went back to town in the fall, they advertised the pig for sale. When a customer showed up, they said to him: "Do you think $6.00 is too much for him? Of course, we paid $12.00 for him when we bought him; but then, we remember we have used him all summer, so we thought $6.00 would be about right."

God's Word, of course, does not improve with age, for it can't; but it becomes more valuable to us, as we make it ours. Handle the Word. That's the way to grow in grace and in the knowledge of the Lord Jesus Christ.

# "That Ye Sin Not"

*"My little children, these things write I unto you, that ye sin not. And if any man sin, we have an Advocate with the Father, Jesus Christ the righteous."*

(1 John 2:1)

That's what God's standard is for the believer - "that ye sin not". There are folks who claim to live sinless lives, and they are often very ready to tell you so.

Like the boy who draws a caricature of some kind and then writes underneath it, "This is a horse." Without the explanation, you'd never know it.

I think of that when I hear a professing believer claim that he or she is living a sinless life. If it were so, everyone would know it immediately; you wouldn't need to tell it.

God knows we don't live without sinning, but He does not lower His standard because we don't live up to it. He wants us, with His help, to aim at sinlessness; and so He set us an example in the perfect life of Christ. Christ is our pattern.

When I was a boy, my father one day gave me a piece of lumber and told me to saw twenty pieces just like that one. But, boylike, I dropped the sample piece he had given me, and cut each next piece by the one sawed previously. When I got through with the twenty pieces, the last was about two inches longer than the first.

Use others for your pattern, and you will get further and further away from your goal. Perfection is found only in Christ.

The story is told of a gentleman who walked into a large museum, where someone was painting a copy of one of those world famous paintings hung there for exhibition. There was quite a crowd around the imitating artist, watching him work. After looking a while, the gentleman walked out, grumbling to himself: "What a crowd! Here stand some fifty pairs of eyes, looking at this cheap imitation, and not one was looking at that marvellous original hanging on the wall!"

But then, all of a sudden, he stopped and said to himself: "You old hypocrite, you are worse than any of them! They were looking at the imitator, and you scorned them. What about you? You were even further off. They were looking at the imitator, but you were looking at the people who were looking at the imitator!"

"But we all, with open face beholding as in a glass the glory of the Lord, are changed into the same image from glory to glory, even as by the Spirit of the Lord" (2 Cor. 3:18). That's the way to become like Christ.

# Perfect Likeness

*"Behold, what manner of love the Father hath bestowed upon us, that we should be called the sons of God: therefore the world knoweth us not, because it knew Him not.*

*"Beloved, now are we the sons of God, and it doth not yet appear what we shall be: but we know that, when He shall appear, we shall be like Him; for we shall see Him as He is. And every man that hath this hope in him purifieth himself, even as He is pure."*

(1 John 3:1-3)

Here in this text is suggested the "matter, the manner, and the measure" of God's love. The Father loves us, as God loves the world. The manner of His love is that He not only has saved us, but has made us His children. The measure of His love is in that, some day, we are going to be just like

Christ Himself. We shall be conformed to the image of His Son.

We are now the children of God, but it is not yet manifest what we shall be. You can't tell, by looking at me, or I at you, that we are sons of God, or rather, children of God.

Often, when walking down a busy city street, someone will rather roughly jostle you; and sometimes I almost turn around and say: "Hey there! Do you know whom you are pushing? Do you know you are pushing a son of God?" They don't, for it is not manifest as yet how I am going to look, but some day we shall be changed into His likeness, in the day of the manifestation of the sons of God, see Romans 8:19.

As you look at a tiny dark seed, so small you can barely see it, it gives no promise of the magnificent flower it is going to produce some day; so the believer, sown in dishonour at death, shall be raised in glory. It is now not yet manifest what we shall be, and so we who know and love the Lord Jesus ought not to expect too much from each other. Remember, we are not yet perfect, though someday we shall be.

Have you heard of the bishop who had a lovely cabin, on an ocean liner, all to himself? But the purser came to tell him that, due to overcrowded conditions, they would have to put another passenger in with him. The bishop strongly resented it, but they insisted, so he said: "Very well; if it has to be, it has to be; but I am going to take a look at my fellow passenger, and if I don't like his looks, something will have to be done about it!"

After a while, he came back, saying: "I guess he isn't so bad, but I don't want to leave my valuables in the room. I don't know whether I can trust him or not. Can you put them in the ship's safe for me?" "Oh, sure," said the purser, "and by the way, your roommate was here a few minutes ago and put his money and jewellery in the safe, too!" He did not like the bishop's looks, either.

And so, you may not like my looks (I don't like them much myself), and I may not like yours, but don't be too critical. We are not always going to be as unprepossessing as we are now.

It is not yet manifest what we shall be. But we shall shine in that glorious future with all the dazzling beauty and glory of our Lord, and be both morally and physically perfect.

# Confession v. Profession

*"Hereby know ye the Spirit of God: Every spirit that confesseth that Jesus Christ is come in the flesh is of God: and every spirit that confesseth not that Jesus Christ is come in the flesh is not of God."*

(1 John 4:2-3)

In these two verses, the second "that" should be left out both times; it is not found in the Greek. It is not a question of confessing or not confessing a fact, but the confession of a Person, the Christ of God. It should read "he that confesseth Jesus Christ come in flesh", or "he that confesseth not Jesus Christ come in flesh".

Note that it is confession which is considered here, not profession, which may be true or false. The Greek word "homologia" means "to say the same thing".

An old Scotch woman cynically used to call signposts "ministers", and when asked why, she said: "Because they point the way, but don't go themselves!" In her estimation, their lips and their life did not say the same thing, so they were not confessors, but only professors.

If you saw signs pointing to the same place, and yet in opposite directions, you would be confused, wouldn't you? When a professing Christian does not practise what he preaches, he breeds only confusion in the minds of people.

They tell the story of a man sitting on a street corner, with the caption "BLIND" on his chest, and with a tin cup in his hand. A passerby kindly dropped a quarter in his cup, but, being a poor shot, it was about to miss the cup, when the blind man quickly shoved the cup under it and caught it.

"Hey, wait a minute!" said the giver. "You are a hypocrite; you're not blind or you would not have seen the coin miss the cup!" "Well, no, sir," said he. "You see, I'm not really the blind man. He got so awfully tired from sitting here that he asked me to take his place a while, while he has gone for a little change." "Where is your friend?" the giver asked. "He's gone to the movies," was the startling reply. They were both hypocrites - professors, but not possessors.

The true believer confesses Christ. He did it for the first time when he confessed Christ as Saviour, as we read in Romans 10:9: "If thou shalt confess with thy mouth the Lord Jesus, and shalt believe in thine heart that God hath raised Him from the dead, thou shalt be saved."

We are to continue confessing Him daily. Strikingly, it says that the unbeliever does not confess Him; it does not say that he denies Him. His silence about Christ is a proof that he does not know or love the Lord Jesus. Therefore, a Christian is supposed to open his lips to speak of his Lord. Silence would put him in the same category as the unbeliever.

In regard to the mere professor and not possessor, it is not what he says about Christ, but what he does not say that marks him as not of God. No true Christian ever preaches from the Word of God without speaking of his Lord and Saviour in some way.

Mr. Spurgeon used to say that if you go to a bakery, and they sell you a loaf made of sawdust, never buy any bread thereafter in that place.

# Preserved and Presented

*"Now unto Him that is able to keep you from falling, and to present you faultless before the presence of His glory with exceeding joy,*
*"To the only wise God our Saviour, be glory and majesty, dominion and power, both now and ever. Amen."*

(Jude 24-25)

This short letter begins with "preserved" and ends with "presented".

Preserved from evil below; presented in the glory above.
Preserved in Jesus Christ; presented by Jesus Christ.
Preserved by mighty power; presented with exceeding joy.
Preserved to be faithful; presented to be faultless.

In between the preservation and the presentation lie justification, sanctification, multiplication (of mercy, love and peace, verse 2), and the daily expectation of His coming.

God multiplies His blessings. I have a typewriter, and the only thing I have against it is that it does not spell correctly. Every once in a while, I find that it misspells words; it transposes letters.

One day, looking at my work, I noticed that it had spelled "multipiled", instead of multiplied. But soon I praised the Lord for the error, for His grace, love and peace certainly have been multipiled - grace upon grace, mountains high.

For successful christian life and service, there is this abundance of mercy, love and peace. Amidst the ever increasing departure from God, we are kept by divine power, preserved in Jesus Christ, while we preserve the faith delivered unto us, verse 3. While others creep (verse 4), we keep.

While waiting for the day when we shall be presented faultless, we must right now be preserved blameless (1 Thess. 5:23). These two are not the same.

Here is a little girl, anxious to help her mother do some sewing. Mother knows her child is incapable of the work, but she gives her a piece of cloth, a needle and thread, and the little girl goes to work. Soon she is tired of the whole thing and is ready to run along. Does her mother blame her? No indeed, the very opposite - she praises her. She tells her how pleased she is that she was so ready to help. But when the child leaves, the mother throws the work aside because it is no good whatever. It is far from faultless, but the child herself is blameless.

Blamelessness has to do with the motives of the heart; faultlessness with the work or the person. We are blameless when we earnestly seek to serve and please our Lord, however faulty our work might be. We shall never be faultless till we are presented in the glory above, with exceeding joy, by our blessed Lord Himself.

I take it that the exceeding joy will be His joy: when, due to His wonderful redemptive work of the Cross, He shall see of the travail of His soul; and when He shall be able to efface forever all sin and stain, all failure and shortcomings, and be able to present us at Court, perfect and immaculate, with the beauty His grace will have put upon us.

What a day that day of presentation will be, when He shall present us to the Father and to all the assembled hosts of heaven as His Bride, lovely beyond all thought - fit companion for the King of kings and Lord of lords!